TOUCHPEBBLES
Volume A

Teacher's Edition

Geoffrey Comber
Howard Zeiderman
Kevin Dungey

CZM Press

Copyright 1994
by CZM Press
48 West Street, Suite #104
Annapolis, MD 21401

All rights reserved. No part of this book may be reproduced in any form whatsoever without prior consent of the authors.

ISBN 1-878461-27-3

Acknowledgements

We would like to thank the following for their help in the publication of this volume:

For *Hound and Hunter*, by Winslow Homer, 1892, oil on canvas. Gift of Stephen C. Clark, ©1994 Board of Trustees, National Gallery of Art, Washington, DC.

For *Portrait of a Clergyman*, by Albrecht Dürer, 1516, oil on parchment. Samuel H. Kress Collection, © 1994 Board of Trustees, National Gallery of Art, Washington, DC.

For *Marchesa Brigida Spinola Doria*, by Sir Peter Rubens, 1606, oil on canvas. Samuel H. Kress Collection, ©1994 Board of Trustees, National Gallery of Art, Washington, DC.

For *The Much Resounding Sea*, by Thomas Moran, 1884, oil on canvas. Gift of the Avalon Foundation, ©1994 Board of Trustees, National Gallery of Art, Washington, DC.

For *Waves at Matsushima*, detail from a six-fold screen, by Sotatsu, from the Momoyama-Edo period, 17th century, color and gold on paper. Courtesy of the Freer Gallery of Art, Smithsonian Institution, Washington, DC.

TABLE OF CONTENTS

LESSONS	INTRODUCTION	
	INTRODUCTION	x
# 1	*A Different Kind of Class*	1
# 2	*The Judge*, A Tale from West Africa	8
# 3	*The Camel and the Jackal*, A Tale from India	13
# 4	*The Clever Thief*, A Tale from Korea	18
# 5	*Hound and Hunter*, by Winslow Homer	24
# 6	*The Lion and the Mouse*, by Aesop	30
# 7	*A Test of Strength*, A Tale from the Fan Tribe of Africa	35
# 8	*Pandora's Box*, A Tale from Greece	40
# 9	*The Confessions*, by St. Augustine of Hippo	45
#10	*Emile* or *On Education*, by Jean-Jacques Rousseau ...	49
#11	*The Pillow*, A Tale from the Middle East	54
#12	*Catching Fish in the Forest*, A Tale from Russia	59
#13	*The Eagle*, A Poem by Alfred, Lord Tennyson	64
#14	*They Share the Work*, A Tale from Latvia	70

#15 TWO PORTRAITS:

    Portrait of a Clergyman, by Albrecht Dürer
    Marchesa Brigida Spinola Doria, by Sir Peter Rubens 76

#16 *The Republic,* by Plato 79

#17 *How to Catch a Thief,* A Tale from China 84

#18 *Definitions of a Straight Line* 89

#19 *Gilgamesh the King,* An Epic from Ancient Persia 95

#20 *The Weapons of King Chuko,* by Lo Kuan Chung 100

#21 *The Odyssey,* by Homer 105

#22 *How Much is a Son Worth?,* A Tale from Saudi Arabia 110

#23 IMAGES OF WAVES:

    The Much Resounding Sea, by Thomas Moran
    Waves at Matsushima, by Sotatsu 115

#24 *About Lying,* by Montaigne 120

#25 *The Man Who Thought He Could Do Anything,*
    A Tale of Native America 125

#26 *Robinson Crusoe,* by Daniel Defoe 130

#27 *Narcissus,* A Story from Greece 135

#28 *The Spider and the Turtle,* A Tale from the Ashanti People of Africa . 140

#29 THE COVER MAP OF ICELAND 146

#30 *The Histories,* by Herodotus 150

INTRODUCTION

I. *GOALS*

The Touchstones Discussion Project reorients students and teachers toward education. From their earliest years in school, students must begin to learn how to teach themselves. It is no longer adequate that our pupils become good students who master particular facts and skills. Skills of a higher order are necessary to flourish in an increasingly technological world. As teachers we should confront this necessity as an opportunity.

It has always been our aim that our students share with us the responsibility for their educations. Yet we have frequently had to subordinate this aim to the specific curricular goals which fill the school day. No sustained effort has been made to direct the emerging curiosity, initiative, and independence of our students toward making them active collaborators in their own educations. However, the emerging professional, economic, and technological world requires that we teachers turn our implicit aim into a reality. This aim is no longer a luxury for a few students but a requirement for all of them. The Touchstones Discussion Project creates a carefully designed environment within which the skills necessary for students to collaborate with us and teach themselves are introduced, practiced, and mastered. It is an environment within which all students, regardless of their apparent ability level, can achieve skills which previously few, if any, students mastered.

The weekly Touchstones class makes collaboration possible by creating an academic environment in which we and our students experience how our interdependence is necessary for the success of the activity. In the Touchstones class, students are not viewed individually as talented or untalented, skilled or unskilled. *All* students have both strengths and weaknesses. They contribute their respective strengths and assist one another to compensate for and correct their respective weaknesses. In addition, the opinions, experiences, desires, fears, and uncertainties of our students animate and bring out the substance in the texts considered. They begin to desire to collaborate with us generally in school because in this specific instance they have had the adequate knowledge and skill to take the initiative in an academic context.

Though participation in weekly Touchstones discussions can instill in students a desire to collaborate with us and each other, a mere desire is not sufficient to achieve serious and sustained initiatives. This step requires incorporating a new set of expectations about their responsibilities and ours, and a new set of skills with which they can achieve these goals. These new expectations and skills, which Touchstones develops, fit naturally with the attitudes of elementary school students. Students have not yet become convinced that they are able or unable to master certain subject matters and skills. We, as teachers, are not completely viewed as the exclusive determiners of class design, goals, answers, knowledge, and skills. Students do not expect to be passive. The model of teaching and learning which will dominate in middle and high schools has not yet structured their expectations. Therefore, the emerging independence of our students can be capitalized on through the Touchstones discussion format. Furthermore, our long-range goal for students—that they someday cease being merely students and become able to teach themselves—can be incorporated into their educational experience. Though discussions will not and should not be the principal method of teaching subject areas, Touchstones discussion classes can create a framework of expectations whose goal is that students learn how to learn, that is, that they learn how to teach themselves.

Learning how to learn is a complex process that requires the development of many skills. Touchstones classes develop crucial aspects of this process through the systematic use of individual and small-group work and through full-class discussion. Though students will learn how to participate in discussions, this important ability is not an end in itself. Rather, in the weekly Touchstones class, students exercise skills that can increase their ability to gain from their regular classes. For example, they learn to

* work with others regardless of background,

* understand what it means to support opinions with evidence,

* take responsibility for their opinions,

* confront new situations comfortably,

* respect other people's opinions,

* respect themselves, and

* listen to, analyze, and think about problems that do not have complete or simple solutions.

These are the kinds of skills we most commonly need in our own lives.

II. *TOUCHPEBBLES*

Touchpebbles is that part of the Touchstones Project which is specifically developed for the elementary grades. This volume, *Touchpebbles: Volume A,* is suitable for grades 2-4. The goals of Touchpebbles are entirely compatible with those of the Project overall, as set out in the section above. Elementary school students, just as much as middle and high school students, need to learn the skills of cooperating, relating evidence to opinions, respecting themselves and others, and in general taking responsibility for their beliefs, their actions, and their educations.

In Touchstones for high schools, these skills are practiced through activities designed to make students explicitly aware of the presuppositions of their own thoughts, of their responses toward the remarks of others, and of their attitudes towards the opinions expressed in texts. Their tendency is to be either contemptuous of the opinions of other people or too accepting of the printed word. These tendencies are checked by exercises that encourage and guide students to view a given opinion as one of many possible views they can entertain in a specific situation. Once the possibility of multiple opinions becomes real for students, they can master the skills of cooperating and listening.

Touchstones for middle schools prepares students for this highly cumulative activity by introducing group discussion, active listening, and active reading. The exercises and class activities in Touchstones for middle schools are more directive and structured but less systematic than those in Touchstones for high schools. Touchstones for middle schools suggests specific questions and lines of approach, while Touchstones for high schools leaves much more initiative to students, both singly and in groups. The middle school approach allows the skills mentioned above to be practiced in a variety of different contexts without requiring students to focus on them directly. In Touchstones for high schools, these same skills are practiced and analyzed exhaustively and self-consciously. The texts in Touchstones for middle schools are also less the focus of attention than they are in the high school program. The middle school texts draw attention to the students' experiences and opinions. In this format, the students learn to discuss and to explore what they had taken for granted. They become motivated learners.

Touchpebbles for elementary schools introduces the skills of active learning through exercises that emphasize the imaginative manipulating, completing, or rewriting of texts. Middle school and particularly high school students are capable of dealing actively with texts by analysis and reflection. Younger students, however, need more tangible devices for doing the same things. Such devices take many forms in the Touchpebbles volumes. For example, in *Touchpebbles: Volume B,* students are asked to complete a text, or to reconstruct a story from parts, or to complete and orient an abstract painting. Each of these activities encourages students to develop an individual point of view. In *Touchpebbles: Volume A* most of the lessons offer two or more perspectives on the same topic, subject, or issue. For example, the lesson entitled *The Eagle* presents a poem by Tennyson and two prose-style versions of the same subject. Basically, the exercises and discussions turn on what is gained and lost by each of the perspectives. In every case, a written text or work of art is actively and cooperatively worked on by students both individually and in groups. Through this work, students begin to explore teaching themselves and each other. They find they have more to contribute than they expected, they learn to work actively with texts, they experience the continual interplay of reasoning and imagining in intellectual exploration, and they realize that the school environment is an integral part of their daily interests and concerns.

III. *THE STRUCTURE OF THE TEACHER'S EDITION*

This volume will enable you to conduct discussion classes in which your students will begin to practice and develop the skills of intellectual initiative and cooperation. This guide for *Touchpebbles: Volume A* is made up of 30 lessons; the first is a preparation for the remaining 29. It is called *A Different Kind of Class.*

Each lesson plan is made up of 4 parts:

1. *Summary/Purpose.* The text is summarized and the purpose of the lesson is set out. In most cases, the specific skills exercised in the lesson are mentioned, and suggestions for discussion are presented.
2. *The Text.* This appears just as in the students' books.
3. *The Student Handout.* This is an exercise that sets the stage for small-group cooperative work.
4. *The Class Activities.* The stages of each lesson are laid out with approximate times, followed by a summary of this information in a rectangular box.

Each lesson involves the students in individual work and small- and large-group discussion. This is done for three reasons. The first is to involve students actively with the texts. The second is to create the opportunity for the extremely diverse skills of the students to contribute to a common activity. The third is to encourage each student to have a sense of responsibility to the whole class.

Students, no less than the rest of us, respond differently to groups of different sizes. Some speak easily in a group of 25-30; others feel more comfortable working and speaking with only 3 or 4 others. Still others are quiet and reserved in groups but work well as individuals. However, in our experience, we find that no student is naturally skilled in discussion. Discussion requires among other things that one express ideas clearly, listen accurately, be willing to change one's own opinions, and respect other opinions. These skills don't develop naturally.

Students who speak readily in large groups almost always have difficulty listening well to what others say. Students who can't read or students who have difficulty speaking in large groups are often very good listeners. It will be your task as the discussion leader to help the students blend their own skills with those of others and to begin to practice new ones. For instance, many students who do well in regular classes often fear being wrong publicly. Since a discussion format on a Touchstones text does not readily lead to a right or wrong answer, but one which is better or worse, such students will often hold back. These students are assisted by the individual and small-group work in the transition to the riskier and more uncertain large-group situation. Other students who try to dominate when in a large group will behave differently in task-oriented, small-group work. This work assists the dominating type of student in learning to cooperate and helps the other students learn not to be intimidated.

These examples should make it clear that normal characterizations of students are not helpful in the Touchstones environment. No student is unambiguously strong or weak, skilled or unskilled. Each comes with assets and liabilities. As the discussion leader, you will learn new things about your students, because they will display aspects of themselves that remain concealed in a regular lecture or question-and-answer class. In addition, the new format will encourage students to adopt new behaviors and sometimes new levels of seriousness which you as a teacher will be able to draw on in regular classes. Below is a chart of student strengths and weaknesses from the perspective of the Touchstones discussion class. The chart alerts you to the types of qualities you as a discussion leader will encourage and others which you will try to modify and shows that, from the vantage point of the Touchstones discussion class, every student has important things to learn.

Strengths and weaknesses of traditionally characterized
students from the vantage point of
Touchstones discussion classes:

The Good Student

Strengths	Weaknesses
Follows teacher's instructions	Expects the teacher to approve remarks
Attends to the text	Does not speak or listen to other students in the context of school
Gives clear and precise answers	Does not expect that answers may lead to further questions
Wishes to reach a correct solution	Is uncomfortable with uncertainty about an issue or problem

The Poor Student

Strengths	Weaknesses
Acts independently of the direction of the teacher	Exhibits behavior in class that can be antagonistic
Thinks often about serious issues like honor, desire, and anger in terms of experience	Tends to dismiss academic learning because it does not deal seriously with issues of interest.
Is not afraid of being wrong	Does not easily receive correction and criticism

The Indifferent Student

Strengths	Weaknesses
Acts as a member of a group	Does not take individual responsibility for actions and opinions
Listens equally well to the teacher and to other students	Does not take initiative for any classroom activity

All these students have strengths and weaknesses. Your task as the discussion leader and the task of each member of the class will be to preserve and improve the strengths and to use others with different strengths to address and overcome the weaknesses.

IIIa. *Individual Work*

In each class students perform individual work using handouts. The handouts for Touchpebbles are usually an invitation to make decisions about a topic or experiment with the text, to modify it, and even to play with it in some productive way. In most regular classes, texts and textbooks are viewed quite differently. They are viewed as containing truths, interpretations, or particular perspectives which the student is expected to learn. On the whole, students are not expected to question or to doubt famous authors. Photos or drawings of people are usually used to show students something historical or factual; and folktales and myths are most often used to reveal the unusual beliefs of another culture or time. Thus students learn that the contents of textbooks are not to be altered or tampered with. To them a mathematics text gives us truths; the folktale provides evidence about unfamiliar people from distant places or times. Therefore, if you alter the text, you probably do violence to these facts.

Because Touchstones has specific educational goals, it views texts quite differently. This volume, *Touchpebbles: Volume A,* focuses on the fact that texts can be viewed from a variety of perspectives. For example, Rousseau's remarks about spoiled children in Class #10 encourage your students to look at their parents in a wholly new way. The familiar sight in magazines, movies, or at a beach of waves rolling onto the shore is shown in Class #23 from two strikingly different perspectives. The handouts in all cases encourage the students to stretch their imaginations and make choices and judgments from points of view which are probably strange to them at first sight. But, as with all opinions expressed in Touchstones classes by the students, they are not clearly true or false, right or wrong. They are best described as better or worse. The absence of right and wrong answers removes the passivity many students adopt when confronted with questions in a school setting. Touchpebbles tries to appeal to the inventiveness of students and their desire to mold things their own way.

IIIb. *The Small-Group Work*

The work of this part of the lesson generally extends the work of the handouts which students complete individually. Having worked alone on the handouts and decided on their responses to the questions, the students need to broaden their perspective. This can be promoted by comparing their individual responses with those of other students. Since the responses are not to be thought of as right or wrong, students will almost certainly respond in very different ways. Therefore, when the students in small groups compare their own responses with other students', they will confront alternative ways of looking at something. This, in turn, will create a situation which you as a teacher can easily use to everyone's advantage. You can encourage them to give reasons why they chose as they did. Furthermore, you can urge them to listen to other opinions and respond to them.

Since the students are in small groups of twos, threes, fours, or fives, they will have far more opportunity to engage in a dialogue which has continuity. Discussions in large groups of more than 20 have a natural inclination to explore varieties of topics for short periods. It requires a great deal of practice and self-discipline for a large group to stay on task and pursue one topic. In addition, all students are likely to find room to talk in small groups. They will not feel threatened. They will be willing to speak their genuine opinions, listen to others, support their own views with evidence, and even change their minds or modify their viewpoints. In short, they will be able to do things in small groups which are almost impossible when working alone or initially when part of the whole-class discussion.

IIIc. *The Whole-Class Discussion*

In Touchpebbles classes, a considerable amount of time and emphasis is on individual and small-group work. This, for the most part, is where the more inventive and creative work is easier to pursue. But ultimately, after the preparation and groundwork carried out in the first part of the lesson individually and in small groups, every student should be made to feel responsible to the class as a whole. The individual and small-group work sets the stage for the more difficult task of large-group discussion. The most simple and effective way to accomplish this transition is to have each small group report on what happened in its session for the whole class to hear and compare with their own experiences. Once that process of reporting has begun, you should feel free to allow students to respond to the reports even as they are being given.

This reporting and responding is the beginning of a genuine discussion. To help them take the step to the real exchange of opinions and a sustained exploration will require your judicious intervention from time to time. The *summary/purpose* and *class activities* sections in each lesson plan will present various routes for achieving this goal. Remember, it is the *skills* of discussion that you need to underscore, reinforce, and model. That is, you should resist criticizing or praising the views of the students. Instead you should invite and encourage them to present reasons and evidence for their opinions. You should concentrate your attention on the presence or absence of discussion skills, such as whether the students are really listening, whether three or four students are speaking at once, whether they fall into side conversations, and whether they disrespect other students. Each problem as it arises can be dealt with in a variety of ways, but the two most useful ways are to draw attention to it directly, or to turn it into a matter of discussion. To draw attention to it directly is to say something like, "I don't think we're listening to what Mary is trying to say. Let's try again please." Alternatively, after several cases where pairs of students are engaged in side conversations, you can ask, "Should we (as a class) allow side conversations? How do they affect the student who is trying to speak? How can we control them?" In other words, you must make clear that there are ground rules for discussions which must be followed and why they are needed. These ground rules are presented in the first class. However, the students will not truly take them seriously until they grasp the consequences of violating them. You should not spare them or protect them from this experience. And, when it happens, you should feel free to encourage the class to discuss the discussion process itself.

IIId. *Opening Questions*

When it is time in the lesson for the whole class to begin the discussion, you will take the lead. A few simple hints may help you in choosing a question to begin the discussion.

1. *Keep the question short.* It should not need any explanation, and it should be easily remembered.
2. *Don't break the question up into two or three parts.* For a discussion, it is confusing to have several alternative directions. That is, the form "Why or why not" is fine for an essay but not for initiating a discussion.
3. *The question should invite responses from the students' experience.* If your question sticks too close to the text, it will greatly restrict the number and quality of responses. "What does the author mean by . . ." cuts the students off from their experience.
4. *The question should be one to which you don't have an answer.* If you have a hidden agenda or answer you're looking for, the students will be aware and assume that you don't really value their opinions.

A few examples may be helpful. Let us consider possible questions for the text of Lesson #9.

Lesson #9 uses a short excerpt from St. Augustine's *Confessions* where Augustine analyzes why he stole some pears when he was a boy. Questions such as "Why do people steal?" or "Why do people do what they're told not to?" or "Is stealing ever right?" allow the students to use their experience or to turn to the text for support. The freedom for them to move in either direction is useful. It maximizes the numbers of possible participants and makes diverse perspectives available. On the other hand, questions such as "Is stealing bad?" or "How can we stop people stealing?" are too unfocused. They encourage the students to take opposing positions and to recount their personal experiences as a mode of arguing. Finally, textual questions such as "Why does Augustine say he stole pears?" force the students to attend solely to the text. Such questions cut the students off from their experience and force them to consider only the written word in front of them.

Let us return to the more general topic of opening questions. When using this present volume, problems about how to begin the general class discussion will be much easier to deal with than you might think. For the earlier parts of each lesson in Touchpebbles, that is, the work with the handouts and in small groups, will lay a groundwork so rich in ideas and opinions generated by the students that the problem of beginning will evaporate. In general, asking what question best begins a discussion is misleading. It gives the illusion that there is one magic question which will result in a discussion. Put this way, it places the burden firmly on the shoulders of the teacher. This invariably results in a question which seeks to unpack the meaning of the text. It is not your responsibility in Touchstones discussions to find the key that unlocks the text's meaning. Rather, your function is to find a question which invites the students to respond so that they share the responsibility for deciding which direction the discussion should take.

IV. *THE ROLE OF THE TEXTS*

The texts in *Touchpebbles: Volume A* are largely non-contemporary and are drawn from many cultures. In addition, paintings have been reproduced. All these share one characteristic which is crucial for a text used in the Touchstones format: each unites within itself the familiar and the unfamiliar, the well-known and the strange. Students may find the issue familiar, but the way it is described or analyzed strange. This role played by Touchstones texts distinguishes Touchstones classes from topic- or issue-oriented classes which may use an accompanying written text, like a newspaper article. These, being entirely familiar, usually provoke debate. Familiarity and unfamiliarity are both equally important in enabling students to discuss, explore, and cooperate.

Each text focuses on a familiar concept, an attitude, or an issue which the students will recognize from their daily experience either in their personal relations or their relations with the social institutions of which they are part. Some examples are *competition, helping another person,* and *learning something.* Students all have a certain amount of experience and expertise in these matters. They therefore will feel they can contribute to a discussion without seeking the approval of an authority, that is, without looking to you, the teacher, or to academically high-performing students.

But the unfamiliar or strange aspect of the text is also important. This unfamiliarity manifests itself through the texts being from a foreign culture or a distant time. Because of this strangeness, students are not immediately clear about the author's account, opinion, or perspective. This encourages students to cooperate with each other in order to understand what is really being claimed. You should encourage this cooperation and resist the temptation to remove the strangeness by explaining things, even if asked.

IVa. *Why Background and Content Are Not Needed*

In a regular content area class, your role as a teacher is usually to account for the unfamiliar elements in texts. Your expertise sets a context so that students can understand material that has a strain of unfamiliarity to it. Often you will supply historical facts or a cultural setting which allows students to get beyond the alien aspects of some text to a kernel which they can recognize. This approach makes perfect sense for certain kinds of educational goals. However, it runs counter to the specific goals of the Touchstones Project. For background information can encourage students to dismiss an alien perspective. Often students are told that a writer held certain unusual opinions because people who lived then or there believed in them. This often means that a lack of scientific knowledge, or particular economic, political, or religious motivations caused the author to hold certain opinions which are not true, but merely prejudices. This approach presents a difference of opinion as a merely external or factual matter rather than something that requires understanding and discussion.

From the perspective of the goals of Touchstones, differences of opinion are always occasions for thinking and exploring. You must continually keep in mind that these texts are tools. No opinion, whether in a text or spoken by a student, is merely silly, absurd, or outdated. If an opinion seems to be like that, then one should try to find a point of view which makes it plausible. This is important because one is thereby forced to become explicit, often for the first time, about one's own opinions and attitudes. Because unfamiliar or strange texts are equally distant from you and all the students, the group has an opportunity to cooperate and to use everyone's skills, strengths, and experiences to make sense of the group's opinions.

IVb. *Why These Texts Are Short*

Touchstones discussion classes differ from those which attempt to deal more directly with issues or topics because Touchstones uses specially selected non-contemporary texts. However, they also differ from other discussion formats which use texts because Touchstones requires no previous preparation. The texts are rarely more than one and a half pages long and are always read aloud in class. Out of a number of reasons for this, the following two are the most important:

i) Reading a text for a discussion class is a skill that requires practice no less than actual participation in a discussion. Students have had no experience in preparing for such classes. At best, they have learned how to read for a regular class where the teacher is the authority, and where questions will be asked for which there are fairly well-defined answers. What is important in such situations is mastering the factual details of a text rather than reading a text to explore its opinions and thoughts. In other words, such texts are prepared for recitation and response rather than for discussion.

ii) Touchstones is intended for students of all abilities and reading levels. Requiring homework would block many students from participation, either because they never prepare for class, because they have reading problems, or because their home situations preclude preparing for class. Yet many of these students can become highly skilled at discussions because they are frequently better listeners than students who are more expert readers.

V. *THE ROLE OF THE TEACHER*

Your role in Touchstones discussion classes will be somewhat different from your role in content area classes, where your purpose is to communicate information and cover material. In Touchstones, you will assist students in the specific exercises given in the lesson plans, create conditions that encourage exploration and cooperative discussions, and monitor the way your students are practicing particular skills. In other words, though you will not be imparting information or opinions, *you will still be a teacher and not an observer.*

Va. *Your Role in Individual Work*

Each lesson is divided into three parts:
1. Individual work.
2. Small-group work.
3. Whole-class discussions.

In the first two stages--individual and small-group work--you will in fact act very much as you might in a regular class. Individual students may have questions, they may not understand some parts of the handouts, or disciplinary problems might arise because students are seated in a circle. You should feel completely free to respond and manage the situation as you would normally. You are not tied to your chair in the circle; you can move around the class to assist or monitor the students.

Each lesson has a *student handout* which is contained in the lesson plans of this teacher's guide. Each student will need a handout sheet. Sometimes the text is read before the students work on the handout, and sometimes it is read afterwards. This will be indicated in the Activities section. Whenever the text for that specific class is to be read, *you* should be the one who reads it aloud. The texts take some effort to understand, and you will be able to read more adequately than any of your students. In addition, if you ask some of your students to be the public readers, not all of them will be able to do it equally well and preferences will be established in the Touchstones environment which could run counter to some of the Project's goals. When it is time for the students to begin their individual work on the student handout, it will often be useful to them if you explain the instructions on the handout. Students who have questions should raise their hands to get your attention. They will not do this in the whole-class discussion but may continue this behavior in these first two stages of the lesson. The principle to keep in mind in the individual work phase is be available when they need assistance, but do not be overly active except in disciplinary matters.

Vb. *Your Role in Small-Group Work*

Your level of activity can and should be greatest in the small-group work. It would be useful for you to spend time with each group during that stage of the lesson. During this work, the small groups will be trying to reach consensus on some question, though in many cases they will not be able to. They will need your help to make this effort and to articulate the problems they face. But it is not your job to bring about consensus. The purpose of the small group is to act as a bridge between individual work and the large-group discussion.

The purpose is not for the groups to reach consensus but rather to make the attempt. The very act of making that attempt involves hearing out the opinions and views of others, practicing how to present one's own view, and articulating points of difference and disagreement. In all these preliminary efforts you can actively assist the small groups.

Vc. *Your Role in the Whole-Class Discussion*

The crucial difference between your role in Touchstones and your role in regular classes will emerge in the large-group discussion. Teachers new to leading discussions often go to one of two extremes. Faced with an interesting text, they try hard—as they do in regular classes— to help their students understand and appreciate the content. Thus, they ask highly textual questions about what the author meant or intended, or questions about the connections and images in the passage. Often at the end of the lesson they will summarize what has been discussed or concluded and frequently spell out their own opinions. In general, teachers are strongly inclined to do these kinds of things in a discussion. In fact, not to have this inclination is to lack respect for your students' intellectual curiosity. However, you must restrain your desire to reveal interesting aspects of the text to the students.

In order for the students to make the discussion their own, they must approach the text through the medium of their own experience. The texts cannot act as tools unless the students acknowledge that the opinions they have about the texts are their own. Only in this way will they take responsibility for the course of the discussion. The students need to learn to take possession of an intellectual activity, to articulate their own opinions, to listen to the opinions of others who disagree with them, to explore together, and to develop intellectual curiosity. Eventually, when they begin to realize that texts can greatly assist them, they will, with your help, make the discussion more textually oriented. However, Touchstones discussions are never merely expositions of a text. Rather, Touchstones seeks an interplay between the text and student's experience and opinions.

When teachers hear this—that they should not interpose themselves between the text and the student —they often tend to the other extreme. When told that this activity is not centered on them, they imagine they are to be mere observers of an activity which will go on without them. In all Touchstones discussions, even in the large-group discussion, *you are always the teacher. The activity will not occur without your continual attention and monitoring.* One of the goals of the activity is to increase the sense of responsibility students feel for the progress of the discussions. As this proceeds, they and you will share the effort of teaching. However, this change occurs gradually and even when it happens you will still be the teacher. On the way toward such a goal, the teacher's level of activity is as high as in a regular class. *The difference between you as a teacher of science or social studies and you as a discussion leader has to do with your focus.* A few examples will help clarify this difference.

Vd. *Two Problems Requiring Intervention*
i) Many Students Speaking at Once

In Touchstones, unlike in regular classes, students speak without raising hands. This naturally leads to situations in which three, four, or more students speak simultaneously. This should not surprise us, for rarely, if ever, have they been in a situation like this. Clearly this is a confusing situation for you and the students. This circumstance requires your intervention. The question is, how should you intervene?

One thing constantly to keep in mind is that discussion skills are difficult to achieve and are best gained when *students* recognize what is needed. Therefore, do not try to avoid or circumvent those problems which make clear the need and utility of certain skills. One such skill is to anticipate the movement of a discussion, to be aware of who is beginning to speak, and to keep in mind the importance both of speaking and of making room for others to speak.

If many students are speaking at the same time, allow that to continue for a short period of time (perhaps 6-10 seconds). Your purpose is to allow them to feel that the discussion format has broken down. At that stage you should intervene if it has not corrected itself and point out that it is impossible to understand anyone with so many people speaking. You might then ask the students to repeat what they were saying and even call on them successively. *Do not feel tempted to introduce hand raising.* In other words, *let them feel the problem, help them solve it with a short-term solution, but expect that the problem will emerge again.* If you find that this particular problem reappears frequently, and it probably will, future interventions will require a different approach. During such a situation, stop the class discussion, describe the problem, and ask the entire class to consider how to go about correcting it. Some students may not see it as a problem and you should permit others to explain why it is and what effect it has on them. When you allow the students to suggest ways to avoid this particular problem, some will want to have you select the speakers. You should then feel free to explain the goals of Touchstones and why that short-term solution would run counter to their learning how to anticipate and make room for one another. In Touchstones, you should not hesitate to make any of the aspects of the process explicit to the students. The more they understand what is happening and why, the more successful the activity will become. However, making the process explicit must be gradual because the students will have to experience the activity before your explanations will make sense to them.

ii) <u>Silences</u>

The previous example involves intervening when the speaking has become chaotic. Another example makes the same point but from the opposite direction, that of unusual silence. Regular classes have occasional silences. Generally, most of the legitimate speaking is done by us teachers either through lecture presentations, explanations, or questions. Silences are rare but can occur. Usually, when we ask a question, four or five hands spring up. However, sometimes our question is greeted by silence. When a silence of 6 or 7 seconds occurs, we are tempted to reformulate our question. In other words, *we* take responsibility for the silence, and *we* make the effort to help the class overcome it. In a Touchstones discussion class, the situation is very different. Silences are part of the fabric of a discussion, and when and how to intervene are determined by different criteria. Sometimes your opening question in a discussion can be greeted by silence, at other times a lively discussion can suddenly stop, or a student may ask a question or make a statement to which no one responds. In each case, you as the leader must decide what to do. In order to decide, you need to keep some of the goals of the Project in mind. Two goals that are relevant are that *students must take possession of the activity* and that *all students should come to see themselves as possible speakers*. In this sense, the silences are not *your* problem and sole responsibility: they are the responsibility of the whole class, and the whole class must be made to feel this and accept it.

A silence in a discussion often lasts much longer than the 6 or 7 seconds in a regular class. Silences of 10 seconds are not unusual, and even 15 to 20 second silences can occur. Neither we nor our students feel comfortable with a 15 to 20 second silence. Though you will feel uncomfortable with such a situation, you should realize that your students will feel even more uncomfortable. Generally, one of them will break the silence. When a student breaks the silence, an important event will have occurred. The student will have acknowledged that the success of the Touchstones activity is not *your* sole responsibility but the responsibility of *all the members of the group*. In addition, often the student who will break the silence will be one who has had difficulty finding a way to enter the discussion. Both of these are positive steps and show that in a discussion a silence can be fertile.

Your attitude toward silence in a Touchstones discussion should be quite different from your attitude in a regular class. Your response is, therefore, also different. You should allow silences of up to 10 seconds before you even consider intervening. If about 15 seconds have passed and the silence is continuing, a decision about intervention becomes necessary. Your first option will be simply to get the discussion moving again. You can do this best by raising a simple question about the text or about the handouts or the small-group work. If the silences continue, you might consider asking your students to write a sentence on what was discussed and have a few students report. In other words, when this situation arises, feel free to move briefly out of the discussion format.

The reasons for class silence are numerous. The students may need some time to absorb and think about what has been said, or they may temporarily have run out of things to say, or they may be bored. If your class is characterized by frequent silences, your intervention will have to acknowledge this third possibility. You may have to ask them why they are silent. This will be a hard question for them to answer. At first, the best they may be able to do is to say they are bored. We have often found that when students say they are bored, they mean either that they do not yet believe they can learn from one another or that the teacher does not give them enough latitude to bring up and explore their own experiences. Because both of these responses will be hard for them to express, you may have to assist them.

VI. *CONCLUSION*

Keep these kinds of issues and concerns in mind as you lead discussions. You remain a teacher who is constantly involved in what is happening but who is not the source of answers. While most students wish to participate in discussions, many habits, expectations, and fears will block them. Your task is to help them get past these barriers and begin to take initiative for the class and responsibility for their behavior and opinions. Teachers can become good discussion leaders without necessarily enjoying participating in discussions. For leading discussions is in many ways a classroom management skill. If you manage your regular classes adequately, you will gradually learn how to apply your particular strengths to the discussion format. However, leading discussions is not merely a matter of technique. In discussion, students are not merely students but people who are undertaking a serious activity. You will thus be able to be with them not only as a teacher but also as a human being. Some teachers worry that this will change the nature of their authority in regular classes. It does! However, our experience shows that the teacher's authority is not diminished. Rather, it stops being merely arbitrary. The teacher's authority is often enlarged by the respect the students begin to feel for someone who is engaged with them in a difficult and serious activity.

Class #1 *A Different Kind of Class*

Summary/Purpose:

Your students and you are about to undertake a new activity—a Touchstones discussion class. In their past classroom experience, you have been the most important person in the room. The students have depended on you for information, for discipline, for calling on speakers, and for covering material. Even in cooperative activities you have set the goals for their tasks. However, in Touchstones discussions your students will gradually learn to take over these functions. Because this is a very gradual process, you will be constantly shifting gears. Sometimes you will act as you do in regular classes by giving them definite tasks and organizing the activity, at other times you will allow them a great deal of room to explore ideas, face problems, and struggle to learn from one another.

The best way to introduce students to Touchstones discussions is to allow them to experience the process. In all cases, a mere list of ground rules is simply too abstract to be helpful. Even if your students understand rules like "do not interrupt others," they will at first be unable to follow them. This is because following them requires the emergence of new habits and skills. The students will acquire these new skills by experiencing the difficulties and problems that arise when the rules are violated and then working out the solutions. This task is itself a valuable educational experience and you should not deprive them of it. You should keep this long-range goal in mind and not feel frustrated in the early stages when problems arise. In these first meetings, your task will be to help them remain patient with themselves, to focus them on the problems, and to assist them in exploring their solution.

The simplest ground rules to use when beginning Touchstones classes are the following:

1. We do not raise our hands when we want to speak.
2. We speak to everyone in the class and not just to our neighbors and friends.
3. We do not interrupt when others are speaking.
4. We listen carefully to what other students say.

The four rules should be written on a large sheet of paper or on a section of the blackboard and kept there. Periodically, even during non-Touchstones activities, you might refer to these ground rules as a way of keeping them before the students. You might use those occasions to talk about the reasons behind the rules. In this activity you will be acting more like a guide than a discussion leader, though you should always be prepared to permit discussion if the students take the initiative. Eventually they will follow the rules and create additional ones because they will have concretely experienced the problems that discussion brings to the surface. This will be an exercise in creating a learning community.

This lesson will not begin with handing out a list of ground rules. Instead, the need for ground rules will be part of the lesson's structure. Today's text contains a partial description of a Touchstones class. Some characteristics of this class are mentioned; others are not and should be brought up by you. For example, the story describes how, in Cheryl's brother's class, students sit in a circle, but it does not mention that they don't raise their hands. That no one raises hands in a Touchstones disucssion is something you should mention to them at the start of today's class. At the beginning of the period, have the students sit in a circle and tell them that you are going to read them a story and that you all will talk about it. Tell them that when they want to talk they should not raise their hands.

The story not only describes the class, it also brings up certain attitudes students have toward such a class. Since the Touchstones class is a different sort of class, students have definite reactions to it. Some students initially object to Touchstones simply because it is different; others respond positively precisely because it is different. Some of these attitudes are mentioned in the story; others could come up in the course of discussion. For example, in the story, two students who are good at giving correct answers are skeptical and scornful about such a class. This is because they get praise and approval under the conventional format where answers are true or false, right or wrong. They are usually able to pick the answer the teacher has in mind. On the other hand, a student who causes problems in regular classes is excited about the prospect of speaking when he wishes.

You should keep in mind that today's meeting is merely their first attempt at a discussion. Students will behave as they always behave and it will take time to create the environment for a fruitful discussion. However, even in this very first phase they are taking on a new form of activity. They are looking at themselves from multiple perspectives, viewing themselves individually as they normally do and yet also trying to see themselves as others do. You should encourage the group to look at themselves as students in regular teacher-centered classes and then compare that with how they would be in a new form of class where they are more responsible for its direction.

A Different Kind of Class (Student vol., p. 3)

About one minute after the bell rang, the students in Mrs. Green's second grade realized today was unusual. Mrs. Green was always in the room when they arrived. But today she was not there. They were there alone. They began whispering to one another hoping someone knew what was going on. Mrs. White, the principal, came to the room and suddenly everyone was quiet. "Students," she said, "Mrs. Green will be late today so I want you to read quietly until she comes." The students tried to read quietly but before long it was noisy again. Tommy, a student who always got himself in trouble, stood up. "If we don't quiet down, the principal will come back and I know I'll get blamed."

"What shall we do?" asked Judy, the student who always knew the answers to Mrs. Green's questions. She was trying to put Tommy on the spot.

"I don't know. Why don't we try to hold class ourselves?" he said, annoyed.

"O.K., I'll be the teacher," said Judy, jumping out of her seat. When the students saw Judy jump up, they began to make noise again, showing her they didn't want her to take over. "If you don't want *me*, then someone else can lead it," she said angrily. No one responded and the whispering began again.

As the noise increased, a student named Cheryl became nervous and spoke up. "I have an idea. My brother is in the sixth grade. In his class, once a week everyone moves chairs into a circle. The teacher reads a story and asks a question. The class then starts talking about the story."

"What do they need to talk about it for?" asked Judy. "Doesn't anyone know the answer to the teacher's question?"

"My brother told me that the question isn't like questions in regular classes," answered Cheryl. "It's not clear if there's just one answer or if the teacher even knows the answer. Her question is mostly to get the group thinking and talking."

"Sounds pretty silly to me," said John, who always raised his hand with answers just like Judy. "That would make it just a lot of people who don't know the answer talking to one another. What's the point?"

"My brother said they talk about their own ideas, get to change their minds if they want to, and find out all kinds of things from one another," said Cheryl, looking directly at John and Judy. "People who seem dumb at first because they don't know the teacher's

3

answers turn out to have really interesting things to say, and some kids who usually know all the answers find out they can learn from other students."

"Sounds great," said Tommy. "You mean it's really not just figuring out the right answer?"

"That's right. The class learns to work together. Everybody has lots of ideas and they help one another. They never know exactly what they'll talk about. Sometimes they talk about what happened in the story, sometimes they talk about similar things that happened to them, and sometimes they talk about their own ideas."

"Why don't we do it?" said Steve, a student who usually never talked in class. "Mrs. Green read us a story yesterday about a judge. We could talk about that. And I have a question to start."

As Steve was about to ask his question, Mrs. Green came into the room. "Sorry I'm late," she said. "What have you been doing?" John quickly raised his hand and when Mrs. Green motioned to him, he said, "We've just been waiting."

"That's not true," said Tommy. "We were going to have a class on the story about the judge that you read to us yesterday. Steve was going to ask us a question and we were all going to talk about it." Others in the class made it clear that they all agreed. Mrs. Green looked pleased and said, "Well, Steve, why don't we? What is your question?"

HANDOUT FOR CLASS #1

1. In the story Cheryl describes her brother's class. Students sit in a circle and talk to each other without raising their hands. Below are some problems that often occur in such classes. Choose the one you feel is the worst problem and put an "x" in the space; choose the one you feel is the least bad problem and give it a "✓".

    _____a) Students sitting next to each other will talk to each other instead of the whole group.

    _____b) Many students will talk at the same time.

    _____c) Some students will talk all the time.

    _____d) Some students will be afraid to talk.

    _____e) Some students will only talk to their friends.

2. Which group would you be in? For example, if you think you might talk too much, you would be in group (c). If you are only willing to talk to your friends, you would be in group (e).

    I think I would be in group_____.

3. Think about the problem you felt was the worst. How could you and your classmates correct that problem? (You don't have to write anything; just think about how you would solve the problem.)

5

ACTIVITIES FOR CLASS #1

1. Ask your students to sit in a circle. You should sit in the circle too. Tell the class briefly that you will read them a story and that they will talk about it with you and with one another. They are not to raise their hands.

2. After you have read the story, ask them to describe the class Cheryl talks about. After they have brought up some aspects, you should mention other characteristics of the different kind of class. This discussion of the text should be focused on these characteristics, though you should give them a great deal of latitude in bringing up differences between this new type of class and regular classes. Then ask them to give their opinions about the attitudes expressed by the students.

3. After about 8 minutes, ask them to complete the handout. You will have to read it aloud and explain what they are to do. They will require about 4-6 minutes to complete the assignment. During this phase you will assist them as you would in a regular class activity.

4. Ask the students to volunteer their responses to the first question. After you have heard the different perspectives, it is especially important for you to have the group consider in turn how each problem could be solved. This will elicit how they have answered question #3. At the end of the class, spend a few minutes going over the ground rules.

(These times are approximate only)

1. Sit in a circle	1 min.
2. Introduce and read text	5 mins.
3. Discussion of text about "new" class	8 mins.
4. Complete handouts (Make sure they understand what is asked.)	5 mins.
5. Discuss answers	15 mins.
6. Present Ground Rules	<u>6 mins.</u>
	40 mins.

Class #2   *The Judge,*
            A Tale from West Africa

Summary/Purpose:

One of the hardest tasks for children and adults is to recognize their own particular interests, desires, and concerns and to control them. All of us, every day, struggle with the differences between what each of us believes or wants to do and what is either true or right to do. *Touchpebbles: Volume A* focuses on these issues and develops skills in students that allow them to distinguish between their own ideas and what is true, and between their own desires and what is just and fair. This is achieved through two routes. The first enables students to become aware that each of us possesses a unique perspective on the world. To deal with many of the texts, handouts, and discussions, they will have to depart from their own point of view and adopt different ones. This will involve exercising their imaginations. The second route will explore how to move from the variety of perspectives to what may either underlie these perspectives, unite them, or be implied by them This will involve students in evaluating evidence, making inferences, and exercising their thought. These skills are necessary for every aspect of their future lives: understanding science and using technology, becoming involved citizens, choosing professions, and acting in cooperation with others. This week's lesson begins this process by highlighting the issues we face and the kind of problems with which we must deal throughout the year. It achieves this by concentrating on the role of a judge.

Though only some of your students will be familiar with judges in courtrooms, either from their own experience or from TV, all of them will have had experience of the role judges play. From their early years they have undoubtedly been involved in disputes and disagreements with siblings and friends that needed the assistance of others to resolve. They therefore have had firsthand experience of how difficult it is to take on any distance from one's own interests and perspectives in order to appreciate another's viewpoint. Usually in these situations they have called upon a parent, another friend, or an adult to assist them in solving the problem or the dispute. This person, who functions as a kind of judge, was probably hoped by each disputant to agree with their viewpoint. Of course it is generally impossible for a judge to agree with both sides. So, even though implicitly, the students gradually came to recognize the function of a judge. A judge is expected to represent what is right, fair, or what is true.

This week's text and handout has the students confront these issues. The story concerns two mice who must divide a piece of cheese. Because they disagree about how to do it, they seek a third person, a judge, to help them. However, the story reveals to them one of the crucial ways in which a judge can be unfair. A judge is expected both to be neutral between the parties in a disagreement and also to be able to separate himself from his own interests and perspectives. In the story, this latter criterion does not hold. The mice were unable to divide the cheese to satisfy each of them. This may have occurred because one side looked more appealing than another, or because they each wanted to cheat and have more than their fair share. Yet, the story shows that the judge may be no better than the two of them. A judge is simply another person and he too may have the same difficulty as the people who disagree: he may want what they want. In the story, the monkey also wants the cheese and finds a way to use his position to get it. The mice are therefore forced to ask themselves why they were not able to settle the dispute without calling in a third person. If each mouse could have appreciated the perspective of the other, they would not have lost the cheese.

This brings up another aspect of asking someone to act as a judge. When there is a dispute, often each person has some merit to his position. It therefore happens that a judge who acts fairly will decide that each party is both right and wrong. Neither will get everything that is desired. Since this is what generally happens, why bring in a judge who may act unfairly and cause both parties to lose everything? In this week's class you should encourage the students to bring up such cases from their experience. You might ask them to describe disputes and disagreements and explain how they dealt with them. The handout will help them focus on these issues by placing them in a similar situation. Each of them is asked to draw a cat. In small groups, some of them are selected to act as judges. The judges will decide which drawings are the best. Afterward they can consider how they chose the judges and what problems judges face. The handout is to be completed before the text is read (see Activities, page 12).

The Judge,
A Tale from West Africa

(Student vol., p. 7)

    Two mice stole a large chunk of cheese. Both wanted to have what they thought was their fair share. But neither of them trusted the other to divide the cheese fairly. So they went to the Lion, the king of all the animals. "King, we want to divide this cheese but we can't do it fairly. We can't agree on what is fair. Please help us." The Lion frowned at the mice because he was very busy but felt it was his duty to help. "I'll send you to the monkey. He's the judge and will help you, but it would be better if you could do it yourselves. Once you bring in a judge many new problems might come up." But the mice wanted the monkey and so the king sent them to his law court.

    The monkey was seated in a big chair behind a large table. The mice asked for his help in dividing the cheese. The monkey said, "Of course I'll be the judge if you want me to." He sent his helper for a scale and a knife. With the knife, he cut the cheese so that one piece was much bigger than the other. Then he ate some of the bigger piece. The mice asked him what he was doing. "I'm eating from this piece so that it will be equal to the smaller piece," he said. He ate so much that when he put both pieces on the scale again, the one that used to be smaller was now bigger. So he began to eat from that piece. The mice now realized that the monkey planned to eat all the cheese. They said, "Give us what's left, O Judge, and we will divide it fairly." But the monkey said, "No. You will fight each other and then King Lion will be angry with me." So the monkey went on eating until all the cheese was gone. Then one mouse turned to the other and said, "Why didn't we trust each other and cut the cheese ourselves?"

HANDOUT FOR CLASS #2

Do not answer question #2 until your teacher asks you to.

Individual Work

1. In the space below, or on the back of this sheet, draw the best picture you can of a cat. (It can be sleeping, standing, sitting, eating, etc. You choose.)

To be completed just before going into small groups.

2. What should the judge for your group be like? Check TWO of these which you think most important.

The judge must be
- ☐ biggest
- ☐ quietest
- ☐ bossiest
- ☐ smartest at schoolwork
- ☐ kindest
- ☐ most thoughtful
- ☐ best at sports
- ☐ strongest
- ☐ your best friend
- ☐ most honest
- ☐ funniest
- ☐ oldest

ACTIVITIES FOR CLASS #2

1. Ask your students to sit in a circle and pass out the handout. The students' first task is to draw a picture of a cat. You should allow them about 8 minutes to do this. The drawing can be in pencil, pen, or crayon.

2. After they have finished, explain that they will go into small groups of 4-5 students. Tell them that in their small groups they will select one from their group to judge which drawing is the best. Before they go into their groups, have them complete question #2 on the handout. You may well have to read each category to them. Then let them go into small groups, select a judge, and ask that student to decide which is the best. This should take no more than about eight minutes. The judge judges his or her picture with the rest.

3. Ask them to form the large circle again and read the story to them. Begin the discussion by asking them when was the last time they needed help to settle an argument. Focus them on what advice they would give the mice. After some reports have been given, have them describe their experiences in small groups. Was it hard to select a judge? How did they pick a judge? Was it easy for the judge to decide? Did they think the judges were fair? Could they have done better deciding as a group on how to choose a judge?

(These times are approximate only)

1. Sit in circle	1 min.
2. Drawing	8 mins.
3. Question #2 on handout	2 min.
4. Small-group work	8 mins.
5. Large group; read story	3 mins.
6. Group discussion	<u>18 mins.</u>
	40 mins.

Class #3   *The Camel and the Jackal,*
                                   A Tale from India

Summary/Purpose:

The opposite of disagreement and conflict is cooperation. If the mice in the last story had been able to cooperate, they would not have needed a judge and would not have lost the cheese. However, cooperation is very difficult to achieve, especially if you don't know or don't like the other person. All too often, someone in the group will try to control or dominate, standing out by being funny or bossy or by finding other ways to resist working with mutual respect. Genuine cooperation requires a realization and recognition of one's own weaknesses as well as one's strengths. It requires a great deal of understanding of oneself and others and a variety of skills and attitudes that will be practiced throughout the Touchstones discussion classes. Some of these skills, such as not interrupting when another student speaks, will be worked on gradually during this year's work. Fundamental attitudes, such as learning that one can only achieve one's own goals when others achieve theirs, will take years to understand and master. In the past two classes, you and your students have probably experienced both disagreement and cooperation. In the case of disagreement, they might have looked to you to judge or mediate. When they cooperated, your role changed. They no longer needed you to resolve their disagreements but rather to assist them in setting goals and in helping them to realize how much they have accomplished. To a great extent, the themes of the texts and the handouts mirror the procedures of the discussion class. The texts are selected so that students have a tangible way to talk about such often abstract issues as cooperation or conflict. Thus, you should feel free to encourage students to use the texts and handouts to analyze their own behavior.

    Cooperation, one of the goals of the Touchstones Project, usually takes place in two different situations. In one case, two individuals have the same goal. In the other case, two individuals have different goals and yet need each other to achieve what each wants. Both forms of cooperation are difficult because they require surrendering one's own point of view and adopting another's perspective. It is easier to cooperate when both people have the same goal, for example, building a fence together which both have agreed they want. However, even when people share the same goal, they must allocate tasks. Deciding who does what can be very difficult. A more precarious kind of cooperation occurs when individuals have different goals and yet need one another to accomplish them. Because they have different goals, it is possible that one will be finished and satisfied before the other. At this point, there is no assurance that the satisfied one will continue to cooperate. This case is presented in this week's text. The two animals don't genuinely cooperate, because the Jackal, having achieved his goal, begins to act purely from his own perspective.

In the story, the Camel and the Jackal are both hungry and need one another to get food. To cross the river to get the food he wants, the Jackal requires the help of the Camel. On the other hand, the Camel needs the Jackal to show him where the sugarcane is. At this stage each needs the other. However, once they reach the other side of the river and find the food, they no longer require one another's assistance at that moment. Their cooperation breaks down. The Jackal no longer thinks of the Camel's needs, nor does he consider the Camel's point of view. Instead, he either intentionally or unintentionally makes enough noise to bring out the villagers who then beat the Camel. When the Jackal and Camel leave, the Jackal once more needs the Camel's help to get back across the river. However, this time the Camel refuses to cooperate with the Jackal and instead gets even by causing him to drown. The question is, did the Camel act properly? For that matter, did the Jackal act properly? Is there any way of accounting for the Jackal's behavior that would encourage the Camel to assist him in spite of his beating?

Cooperation typically breaks down in discussion classes and in many daily activities. A period of cooperation ends among people or groups, and it becomes necessary to decide whether any future cooperation is still possible. The Jackal and Camel would probably agree on the facts of the case—the Camel was beaten because the Jackal howled and yelped. However, the two animals would probably disagree over why the Jackal did it. The Jackal claims he did it because of a habit; he didn't decide to cause the Camel pain. The Camel either doesn't believe the Jackal's explanation or believes it doesn't matter. Because he was hurt, he will take revenge. In the handout, the students reconsider this situation. They are to decide how they would respond to being hurt and whether there are any circumstances that might make future mutual cooperation possible. In other words, if someone hurt them by accident or without thinking, could they still cooperate? In addition, you should ask them whether the Camel and Jackal could cooperate again if the Jackal did what he did by accident or without thinking. What if the Jackal did what he did on purpose? This is a case that occurs after a war. Can enemies ever work together again?

The Camel and the Jackal, (Student vol., p. 9)
A Tale from India

    A Camel and a Jackal, an animal who is like a small wild dog, met one day and talked about what they liked to eat. The Camel said he liked sugarcane, and the Jackal said he liked fish and crabs that he got from the river's edge. The Jackal said, "I can't swim. But if you carry me over that river, I'll show you where there is sugarcane, and I'll have fresh fish and crabs."

    The Camel agreed, so he swam across carrying the Jackal on his back. The Jackal showed the Camel where the sugarcane was growing, and they both began their meals. But because the Jackal was much smaller than the Camel, he finished his meal of fish and crabs before the Camel had eaten three or four mouthfuls of sugarcane. The camel was still very hungry.

    As soon as the Jackal had finished, he began running all over the sugarcane field, howling and yelping as loudly as he could. The local villagers awoke and thought animals were in their fields stealing crops. They hurried out and found the Camel eating their sugarcane, but the Jackal had hidden. They caught the Camel and beat him half to death.

    When the villagers had left, the Jackal came out of hiding and said to the Camel, "Let's go home."

    The Camel said, "Jump on my back and I'll swim back across the river." When they were in the middle of the river, the Camel said, "That was selfish and mean of you to howl and yelp after you finished your dinner. I had barely started my dinner when the villagers came and beat me with sticks and whips. Why did you make such a noise?"

    "I don't know," said the Jackal. "It's just something I always do. It's a habit. I always sing and run after a good meal."

    The Camel said, "How strange! I have a strong need to roll over in the water whenever I'm swimming."

    "Oh, no!" cried the Jackal. "Why?"

    "I don't know," replied the Camel. "It's just something I always do. You know, it's a habit." So he rolled over in the water. The Jackal fell off and was drowned, but the Camel swam to the opposite shore.

HANDOUT FOR CLASS #3

1. One person hurts another. The person who is hurt doesn't know if it was done on purpose, or without thinking, or just by accident. What should the person who was hurt do about it? Check the best thing to do with ✓. Check the reaction you think is the worst with ✗.

    _____a. get angry, but do nothing.

    _____b. get angry and get back at them later.

    _____c. get angry and hit them.

    _____d. tell them they're angry and not to do it ever again.

    _____e. ask them why they did it.

    _____f. (some other reaction that you suggest.)

2. Hurting someone is probably bad. Which is worse: when someone hurts another person without thinking or by accident?

    ☐ without thinking   ☐ by accident

Answer this question when your teacher tells you to.
3. Did the Jackal run around, yelp, and howl on purpose or without thinking?

    ☐ on purpose   ☐ without thinking

ACTIVITIES FOR CLASS #3

1. Ask your students to sit in a circle and pass out the handout. Have them complete questions #1 and #2.

2. Read the story to them and ask them whether it was right for the Camel to do what he did. You might well want to bring up other cases or encourage them to recount cases where they or someone they know well got even with someone and what happened as a result. This part of the class should last about 10 minutes.

3. Have them next answer question #3 on the handout. This focuses them on the reasons which might explain why the Jackal acted as he did.

4. After they have completed the handout, place them in small groups of four or five. Each group should be made up of students who gave the same answer to question #3. These small groups are to decide how the Jackal could convince the Camel to help him get back across the river. They should have about eight minutes for this task.

5. Bring them back into the large group and have each group report on what they decided.

(These times are approximate only)

1. Form circle	1 min.
2. Complete handout questions #1 and #2	2 mins.
3. Read story and discuss	14 mins.
4. Complete handout question #3	1 min.
5. Small-group work	8 mins.
6. Group reports	14 mins.
	40 mins.

Class #4   *The Clever Thief,*
                           A Tale from Korea

Summary/Purpose:

Regular classes place a premium on correct answers. We teachers try to communicate facts and ideas to students and gauge how well we have succeeded by their answers in classes and on tests. Touchstones discussion classes are quite different. Your concern is not to cover the material in the texts or in the handouts. Rather, your main task in these classes is to develop student skills and foster new intellectual and behavioral habits. In other words, your students, in addition to increasing their pool of information, will change at deeper levels. These changes will make all of your students more able to gain from you in regular classes. Students will learn to share responsibility with you for their own educations. But to achieve this requires a fundamental change in attitude about themselves. All fundamental change is difficult and requires comparing our own opinions about ourselves with what others say honestly about us. This is especially hard when what is said is critical of our own thoughts, manner, or ideas. In the previous class, students had to put themselves in someone else's place. In this class, they will practice listening to and exploring what others think of them.

All of your students are familiar with certain ways in which they have changed over the past few years. They probably remember how they misbehaved when they were younger and how they have changed. Being embarrassed, fearing being mocked or made fun of, being accused of acting like a baby, all these are powerful motivators for changing behavior. In many cases, these changes in their behavior or attitude occurred because they came to see themselves as others whom they respected, loved, or feared saw them. Deciding to change involves not just adopting a point of view that is different from their own but indeed one that directly criticizes how they are behaving. This ability to accept criticism is fundamental to all true learning. The typical expression of this recognition is to feel shame. When we feel ashamed of ourselves, we are acknowledging two views of ourselves. One view is how we presently are and behave; the other is how we wish we could be, and, at least at the moment of feeling shame, how we aspire to become. The class will begin to consider these issues with this week's text and handout.

The story tells about a thief who finally gets caught. While he is in prison, he begins to regret his life and wishes to change. For the thief, this resolution emerges from his own experiences in prison. He devises a plan to free himself, return home, and live a different life. His plan involves confronting the rulers of his country and showing them that, if they could see themselves from a new perspective, they would see that they are no different from him. He presents the king with what he claims is a magical plum pit. He says it will produce golden plums if planted by someone who has never cheated or stolen. The king and his ministers do not accept it. All of them, especially the king, remember times when they too stole or cheated. The king feels shame and frees the thief in gratitude for the lesson he has learned. That feeling of shame was, according to the king, a precious gift. In the class discussion have the students focus on whether they feel this was indeed a precious gift. The handout reinforces this question by asking them to describe how they could be a better member of the discussion group.

The handout first presents the students with a list of typical ways people behave in discussions. Some students talk too much, others are too shy to speak. Student are asked to check what most accurately describes their own behavior. To do this, each student must reflect on his or her own past performance in class. Some of the judgments they are asked to make about themselves are quite strong and critical. For example, "I talk too much" or "I interrupt people." But they should be able and willing to do this. Then the students are paired. Before the pairs of students begin any discussion, each student completes question #2 of the handout. The judgments in question #2 are purposely much less harsh or critical than those in question #1, for they are judgments about their partner, not themselves. The students, still in pairs, then compare and discuss the judgments, and try to agree on which best describes each of them. This activity forces them at least to consider and respond to a different perspective. After they have done this, read the story to them. You might begin the discussion of the story by asking whether they think the king will change and why. In the course of the discussion refer back to the handouts and the paired activity. You can ask them if they discovered anything new about themselves and how they will go about changing.

The Clever Thief, (Student vol., p. 11)
A Tale from Korea

Many years ago there was a thief who had never been caught by the police. He grew rich but, because he thought he was so clever, he became careless. One day he was caught stealing some spices from a shop. He was arrested and sent to jail. He kept trying to escape, but the prison was so strong that he finally gave up. For a year he sat in his cell. At first he just regretted his carelessness, but then he began to feel that he had wasted his life and wished he could begin again. He thought about all the rich and powerful people in his country and how he could have been one of them if he had not chosen to be a thief. As he thought about what the king and the other powerful people in his country were really like, he made up a plan to get out of jail. However, he promised himself that if he succeeded he would live a quiet, honest life.

The next day he told the jailer that he needed to see the king. He said he had a great gift for him. Startled by the request, the jailer took the prisoner to the royal palace. The king was on his throne surrounded by his helpers and his generals. When the king asked him what he wanted, the old thief said he had a great gift for him. "If you waste my time," said the king, "I will have you killed." "I have a wonderful gift for you," said the thief and presented a beautifully wrapped box to his ruler. The king opened the box and found a plum pit. "How dare you waste my time and bring me something so ordinary," said the king.

"My king, this is a very special pit. The person who plants it will reap golden plums." The king became interested but asked, "Why don't *you* plant it?" "That's the sad part of it," said the old thief. "Many years ago I stole it, but it only works if planted by someone who has never stolen or cheated. That is why I have brought it to you." The king shook his head sadly and remained silent. He was an honest man but remembered how he had once stolen a few pennies from his mother when he was a child. "What about some of your helpers or generals?" asked the thief, looking at the important people surrounding the king.

None of them answered because they all remembered that they had used their power to steal and cheat others at some time in their lives. The room remained silent until finally the old thief said, "You all cheat and steal and yet *I* am sent to jail for stealing a few spices in the market. In fact, I am better than you are because at least I know I am a thief and have become ashamed of myself." The king lowered his head for a moment in shame. "Sir, you are free. You have in fact given me a wonderful present. Sometimes kings and powerful people forget that we are just like everyone else. We will remember the lesson you taught us." The thief was pleased at this result but wondered whether these rulers would learn this lesson. Still, he returned to his home to fulfill his promise to himself to live a quiet and honest life.

HANDOUT FOR CLASS #4

Answer this about yourself. Do not answer question #2 yet.

1. Make a check by the item that best describes how you are in your Touchpebbles discussion class.

    _____ I talk too much.
    _____ I don't talk enough.
    _____ I interrupt people.
    _____ I only listen to people I like.
    _____ If people don't like what I say, I am unhappy.
    _____ I talk to my neighbors.
    _____ I try to help other people talk.
    _____ I admit when I'm wrong.

Answer this one about your partner.

2. Make a check by the item that best describes how you see your partner in Touchpebbles discussions.

    _____My partner should speak more.
    _____My partner needs to listen more carefully.
    _____My partner should help others speak.
    _____My partner needs to let others finish talking.
    _____My partner should let other people speak more.
    _____My partner should try harder to listen to everyone who speaks.
    _____ My partner shouldn't be unhappy if others don't like what he or she says.
    _____My partner needs to admit when he or she is wrong.

ACTIVITIES FOR CLASS #4

1. Have the students sit in a circle and pass out the handout. Ask them to complete question #1. You may wish to start this session by asking them whether these behaviors have in fact occurred in the first three classes. This part of the class should take about four minutes.

2. Pair the students (one group may have three members) and have them answer question #2 about their partner. In pairs the students need to consider and compare their responses about themselves with the judgments of their partner. They should try to agree on one item for each member. This should last about five minutes.

3. Place them in small groups of five to six students and have the group consider how each of them can be a better member of the discussion group. In other words, they need to consider how each of them needs to change.

4. Read the text and open the discussion by asking whether they think the king will change. Why or how?

(These times are approximate only)

1. Sit in circle	1 min.
2. Handout, question #1	4 mins.
3. Pairs, question #2	5 mins.
4. Small-group work	8 mins.
5. Read text and discuss	<u>22 mins.</u>
	40 mins.

Class # 5   *Hound and Hunter,*
                          by Winslow Homer

Summary/Purpose:

*T*ouchpebbles: *Volume A* is generally concerned with developing the skills of understanding different perspectives and articulating them. In its most common meaning, perspective describes a technique used in certain works of art. In late 14th-century Italy, a new style of painting emerged, initiating the period we call the Renaissance. In this form of painting, *how* we actually see things in the world took on an importance that it had earlier held among the Greeks but that it had not held during the intervening 1800 years. When we look at any object, how we see it depends on our position. People looking at the same object from different positions see it differently. By studying these differences, painters were able to paint good approximations of how we actually see things in the world.

Since that time, the term perspective has extended its meaning. It not only means seeing an object differently but covers the entire range of differences in intellectual attitudes and beliefs that people have about particular subjects, issues, or the world itself. Just as visual perspective depends on the physical position of the viewer's eye, intellectual perspective depends on the cultural, economic, social, and educational position of the thinker. In this class, students will explicitly discuss the differences between visual and intellectual perspective.

To do this, we use a painting by Winslow Homer. Have the students look at the painting before they complete the handout. They will be able to identify many objects represented. The dog, the young boy, the deer, the boat, and the shoreline. Have them concentrate on the spatial relations among the objects: how far is the canoe from the dog and from the different parts of the shore? You might have them attend to any other relations they notice, such as the size of the canoe or the dog. This will give them some practice in "reading" how objects are represented in pictorial space. You might also have them compare the geometric center of the painting (approximately ¾ inch to the left of and slightly above the boy's eyes) with the visual center, which is a triangle whose three vertices are the heads of the boy, the deer, and the dog.

In the handout, they are asked to make some decisions about the painting, such as the season of the year, and the attitude and expression on the boy's face. This activity gives them some practice in interpreting the content of the painting and sets the stage for the principal activity of the class. In small groups they are to create a story about the painting. What is the boy doing? How did the deer get into the water? Is the deer dead or alive? What is the dog doing, or any other questions you or they might ask. These stories will undoubtedly differ from one group to the next. You should give them enough time to report their stories to the large group, provide the evidence for their versions, and have the class comment on the differences.

    This meeting will therefore raise the issue of perspective in two aspects, the visual and the intellectual. One question the class could confront is the difference between the two class activities. Weren't they better able to agree on certain visual aspects of the painting than to decide what particular narrative was correct? Why should this be? Why is there more uncertainty about the content of the painting than about the spatial relations among the various objects? In addition, if you feel it is appropriate, you might ask them whether their stories about the painting told as much about them as about the painting.

HOUND AND HUNTER, (Student vol., p. 15)
by Winslow Homer Color reproduction appears in student volume.

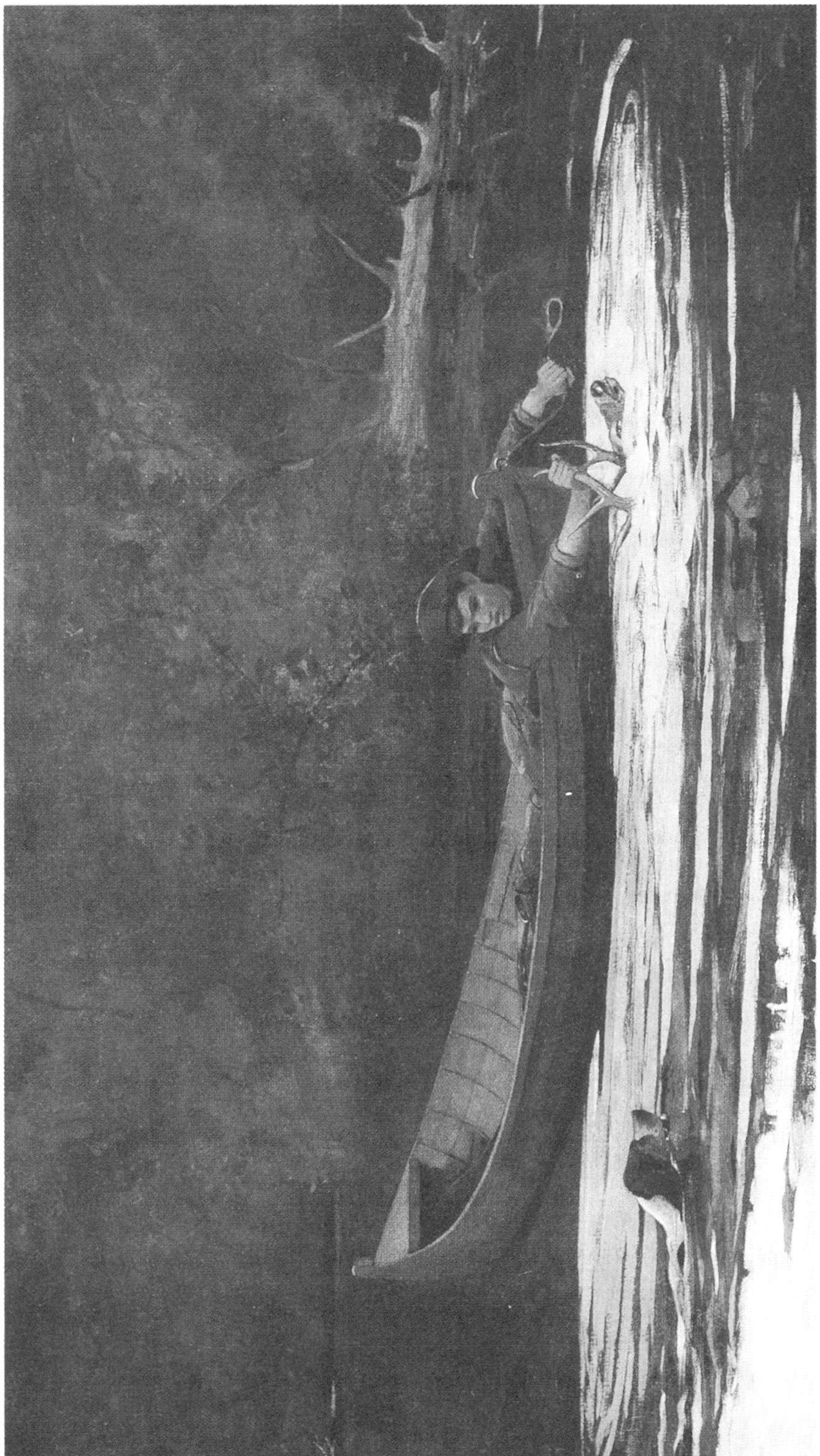

HANDOUT FOR CLASS #5

1. Look at the painting for a few moments, then try to answer these questions.

    1. Is the river flowing ☐ left to right, ☐ right to left?

    2. Is the deer ☐ dead, ☐ wounded, ☐ struggling, ☐ swimming?

    3. Is the boy ☐ angry, ☐ sad, ☐ excited, ☐ pleased?

    4. Is the dog ☐ helping the boy ☐ helping the deer ☐ watching the boy?

    5. Is the boy ☐ helping the deer ☐ calling the dog ☐ catching the deer for supper?

    6. Is the weather ☐ cold ☐ warm ☐ going to rain ☐ sun coming out?

2. In your group, compare your answers and agree about them. Then make up a story together and pick someone to write it down. Be sure to give the boy and the dog a name in your story.

ACTIVITIES FOR CLASS #5

1. With all the students sitting with you in a circle, have them look at the picture. Begin by having them identify as many things as they can, such as the dog, the boy, the deer, the log on the shore, and so forth. Then ask how far apart things seem to be from each other: how far away is the dog from the boy? how far is it to the shore? is the dog closer to the boy than the shore? Ask them where they tend to focus their attention. At this point you could show them the geometric center of the painting (found at the intersection of the diagonals drawn from the corners) and have them compare that with the triangle of action formed by the heads of the boy, the dog, and the deer.

2. Pass out the handouts to each student, give them a minute more to look at the painting and then ask them to answer all the questions. Tell them that they are going to write a story about the painting.

3. Divide the class into small groups (3-4 each) and tell them to compare their answers and agree on an answer for each question. They should also pick one person (or the person may volunteer) to write the story that the group makes up together. Tell the group that they must have evidence from the painting to support their story.

4. After 15 minutes, bring them back to the large circle and ask each group to read its story. Allow students to comment on the differences and to hear evidence from the painting for the different story versions. If a discussion of the painting begins, allow it to go on, but make sure that each group reads its story. Can students come up with any way to decide which version is best?

(These times are approximate only)

1. Sit in circle; look at painting	5 mins.
2. Fill out answers to question #1	5 mins.
3. Small-group work: compare answers	5 mins.
4. Small group writes story (question #2)	12 mins.
5. Small group reads stories; discussion	<u>13 mins.</u>
	40 mins.

Class #6 *The Lion and the Mouse,*
by Aesop

Summary/Purpose:

All of your students differ from one another. At almost any age that we study people we find large differences in their skills and interests. In school we teachers notice that certain students read, or write, or speak, or calculate, or remember, or listen better than others. The students are also aware of these differences. Often they say about themselves that they are good at and like certain activities, or that they are bad at and thus don't like certain others. These two claims frequently go together, though one need not always precede the other. Students who read well generally enjoy reading; people who enjoy working with numbers very often become good at mathematics. As a general rule, we find that people like what they're good at and that they are good at what they like. The opposite is, unfortunately, also all too frequently the case. This negative self-assessment blocks many of our students from making the progress they might; for often they minimize the importance of what they don't like or aren't good at yet. This, in turn, causes them to avoid the effort required to break out of this cycle. Touchstones is intended to avoid this impasse by building a bridge from the skills they possess to the skills they lack and by recognizing the importance and mutual interdependence of many different kinds of skills.

From the vantage point of Touchstones discussion classes, no one is generally skilled or unskilled at discussion prior to any experience in the Project. This is because none of your students have any systematic and sustained experience at true discussion. In addition, each student, no matter how successful, will bring strengths and weaknesses. For example, highly articulate children often have difficulty listening to others. On the other hand, students who are behind in reading skills are often very sensitive listeners. The overall success of the class will depend on students recognizing the skills they have as well as those they lack and realizing that they need both. This can be very difficult. A good reader who listens poorly to others probably also imagines that most others are not worth listening to. A poor reader who listens well probably imagines that no one cares what they think. Their perspectives on themselves and others will have to be broadened. They will have to realize that they need one another. Eventually they will have to exert themselves in Touchstones classes to develop the skills they lack. The text and handout will enable the students to explore this issue.

The fable by Aesop, *The Lion and the Mouse,* is a classic example of this problem. The lion, the king of the jungle, is acknowledged by all the other animals to be the most powerful and skilled of them all. The lion can represent students whose already clearly developed talents and skills are recognized by teachers, family, and friends. The mouse who appears to have no important skills can represent those students whose latent talents and abilities have not been recognized by anyone, possibly even themselves, though in the story the mouse seems to feel confident that he can help the lion at some later date. However, the lion changes his opinion only when forced by a life-threatening situation to recognize the competence of the mouse. Clearly, all of us, your students included, need to learn this general lesson without dwelling too much on the unusual circumstances of the story.

The handout asks them to assess a list of activities based on whether the students are good at them or not. They are then asked to pick one thing they are not good at but would like to learn. In small groups, they will discuss how they would go about becoming good at this activity in which they perceive themselves to be weak. In many cases, the information on how to improve will come from some other person who in fact possesses the skill they'd like to have. This person will not infrequently be someone they don't know very well. Thus, they can begin to recognize the variety of skills distributed among their classmates. This will assist them in learning how to respect one another. Significant change begins when someone can imagine being different.

The Lion and the Mouse,   **(Student vol., p. 17)**
by Aesop

Once a lion was lying asleep in the long grass near a river. A mouse who was hurrying home didn't notice him. The mouse brushed against the lion's whiskers and ran across his paw. The lion was a light sleeper. He was always ready to attack, even while sleeping. At the stirring of his whiskers, he awakened and caught the mouse with his other paw. He was about to make an end of the tiny creature who had disturbed him. However, he heard the mouse speak to him respectfully. "O King, forgive me. I didn't mean to interrupt your rest. I was hurrying so I didn't notice where I was going," said the mouse.

"And why should I care? You were careless and there are no second chances in the jungle," answered the lion.

"O King," answered the mouse, "if you let me go, I shall be grateful forever. Perhaps one day I will be able to help you."

The lion was so surprised at the mouse's reply that he roared with laughter. "You help me! A tiny mouse help the King of the Jungle! Impossible! But what you say is so funny that I'll let you go," and the lion lifted his paw and allowed the mouse to continue home.

A few weeks later the mouse was again returning home, when he heard a noise in the bushes. He was surprised to hear the lion roaring in pain. He inched closer to the sound and soon saw the reason. The lion was caught in a net set by hunters. The ropes surrounded him and each time he moved they were drawn tighter. "Lion, O King, don't move. You're only making it worse. I'll be right there." The lion heard the mouse and looked ashamed at how careless he had been. "Now is your chance to laugh at me," said the King of the Beasts.

The mouse replied, "Lion, you once saved my life. I am forever grateful to you." At that the mouse began to chew away at the ropes and before long was able to cut through the net. The lion was amazed to see how clever the little creature was. When the hole was large enough to escape, the lion jumped forward and then paused in front of the mouse. "Thank you, Mouse. You really were able to help me," he said, as he looked at his tiny helper and then leapt into the forest.

HANDOUT FOR CLASS #6

1. All of us have some things we are good at and some things we can't do or find difficult. Listed below are many different kinds of skills. Mark those you are good at (✓); mark those you are not good at (✗); mark those you don't care about (○). Be sure you mark at least one with (✓) and one with (✗).

	Good at it	Not good at it	Don't care
a. Doing arithmetic	☐	☐	☐
b. Speaking so that people understand me	☐	☐	☐
c. Running fast	☐	☐	☐
d. Helping others with chores	☐	☐	☐
e. Writing neatly	☐	☐	☐
f. Writing stories	☐	☐	☐
g. Keeping secrets	☐	☐	☐
h. Telling stories	☐	☐	☐
i. Playing a team sport	☐	☐	☐
j. Keeping my room clean	☐	☐	☐
k. Getting along with people	☐	☐	☐
l. Listening and remembering	☐	☐	☐
m. Making people laugh	☐	☐	☐

2. Look back over the whole list above in #1 and pick the one that you would most like to be good at. Discuss in a small group how you could become good at it. If someone in your group happens to be good at the thing you'd like to learn to do well, you might ask them how they learned to do it.

ACTIVITIES FOR CLASS #6

1. Ask all the students to sit in a circle. Pass out the handout. Have them answer question #1.

2. Put them in groups of 4 (5 if necessary) and have them discuss briefly with each other what they see themselves as good or bad at. Encourage other members of the group to say whether that self-assessment seems accurate. After some time spent comparing their impressions, ask them to move on to question #2. Each student should have a turn to say what they would like to be good at. The group will help them figure out how they might accomplish it.

3. After 15 minutes total in the small group, have them return to the large group. Read the story to them and have them read it silently. The story gives an instance where the mouse helped the lion. Ask them how in the future the two animals could help one another. After they have considered this for a few minutes, turn their attention to the discussion class itself. Ask them what abilities they think people should have for a successful discussion class. Ask them whether they think that listening is as important as speaking. After they have discussed this for a while, bring them back to the story by asking them what they think the lion learned.

(These times are approximate only)

1. Sit in circle and pass out handout	3 mins.
2. Fill out question #1 on handout	5 mins.
3. Small-group work, question #2	15 mins.
4. Read the story and discuss	<u>17 mins.</u>
	40 mins.

Class # 7 *A Test of Strength,*
A Tale from the Fan Tribe of Africa

Summary/Purpose:

In the previous meeting, your class explored how they were different, how they each had different skills and weaknesses, and how they might use other people's skills to compensate for their own limitations. An important question emerges out of these considerations: are we equal in spite of our differences? The claim that we are equal is the fundamental tenet of American society as manifested in our Declaration of Independence and our Constitution. However, this claim is very difficult to reconcile with the realities of our daily lives. What prevents our recognition of the truth of this claim is the overwhelming fact of our differences. For it is almost impossible not to notice how we are different and thus to rank certain individual characteristics as more or less valuable and important. One of the results of the belief that we are equal is that we treat one another with genuine respect. The consequence of the belief that we are not equal is that we disrespect one another.

In the Touchstones meetings you have probably had this concern very much on your mind. Clearly, in the early stages of any discussion group, friends principally pay attention to what their friends say. They often ignore what students they don't know or don't like have to offer. This is not surprising, because friends respect one another and believe that they are basically equal. It's hard to imagine real friendship occurring between people who do not respect one another and who do not feel they are equal in spite of their differences. However, what may very well have happened in the Touchstones class is that your students have begun to learn new things about each another. They may in fact have started to surprise each another. Often a student will find that someone they haven't liked or known says something that is helpful or interesting. Gradually a feeling of respect emerges. To achieve this respect requires that they reconceive various characteristics of the other person. Some qualities of behavior which bothered them in the past, before they came to respect this person, they might well view quite differently. In today's class the handout will set the stage for reconsidering others by helping them see how they themselves are different from and the same as those they already respect, their friends.

The handout presents a list of characteristics, such as height and interest in music, and asks how important it is that their friends share these characteristics. For many of the students, this will be the first time they have ever directed their attention to this sort of question. They have probably developed their friendships implicitly and thus have not realized that they may have been using various criteria. They could well be surprised at what they consider important and unimportant about their friends. Some of the students will probably think some characteristics that are not on the list are more significant in their friendships, such as whether someone is kind or nice or a good person or honest or just fun to be with. You should give them the opportunity to bring these up. In the story the situation is reversed. A turtle claims to be friends with a hippo and an elephant. Both laugh at him because they are so different from him. The turtle then suggests a test of strength between himself and each of them. By tricking the hippo and elephant, the turtle convinces them that he is equal to them in strength and becomes their friend. The story questions whether the turtle is indeed their equal. Of course in the story, the turtle is not their equal in strength. Rather he tricks them into believing that. But does the turtle's cleverness make up for his lack of strength so that, even though they are different, they are nonetheless equal? You should invite the students to investigate whether friends must be equal and, if so, how.

A Test of Strength, (Student vol., p. 19)
A Tale from the Fan Tribe of Africa

The Turtle thought he was very wonderful. Wherever he went he always would say, "We three, the Elephant, the Hippo, and I, are the greatest animals in the jungle. We three are equal in power and strength." When the Elephant and Hippo heard this claim, they both laughed. The story of their laughter got back to the Turtle and angered him. "So, they laugh at me! I'll show them my power. Before long they'll realize that I'm equal to them. Soon they'll think of me as a friend."

The Turtle went into the jungle to find the Elephant. "Elephant, my friend, I am here to visit." "You're not my friend," said the Elephant. "You're too small and weak to be my friend." "Elephant, don't get angry. Let's meet tomorrow and have a test of strength — a tug-of-war. We will both tug at the ends of a vine. If I move you, I am the stronger. If you move me, then you are the stronger. If neither of us moves, we will be equal and we will be friends." The Elephant thought the test was silly but agreed. So the Turtle got a very, very long vine and gave the Elephant one end. "Tomorrow, when you feel the vine shake, we will start pulling and neither sleep nor eat until the test ends."

Then the Turtle went to see the Hippo and the same thing happened. The Hippo did not want to be called the Turtle's friend but agreed to the tug-of-war. He took the other end of the very, very long vine.

Early the next day, the Turtle went to the middle of the vine and shook it. The Elephant grabbed his end and the Hippo grabbed his end, and the tugging began. Each pulled at the vine with all his strength and it remained tight. At times, it moved a little toward the Hippo, and then a little toward the Elephant, but neither could pull the other very far.

The Turtle watched the tightened vine. Then he went away to look for food, leaving the two at their contest.

Late in the afternoon, after eating and resting, he rose and said, "I will go and see whether those fools are still pulling." When he got back the vine was still stretched tight with neither of them winning. At last, Turtle cut the vine. The vine parted, and at their ends the Elephant and the Hippo, so suddenly let go, fell with a great crash back onto the ground.

The Turtle started off with one end of the broken vine. He came to the Elephant who was looking sad and rubbing a sore leg. Elephant said, "Turtle, I did not know you were so strong. When the vine broke I fell over and hurt my leg. Yes, we are really equals. Strength is not because the body is large. From now on, we will call each other friend."

Most pleased with this victory over the Elephant, Turtle then went off to visit the Hippo, who looked sick and was rubbing his head. The Hippo said, "So, Turtle, we are equal. We pulled and pulled and even with my great size I could not win. When the vine broke I fell and hurt my head. Indeed, you are certainly as strong as I am. We will call each other friend."

After that, whenever these three got together with others, the three sat together on the highest seats. And always they addressed each other as friend.

Do you think they were really equal?

HANDOUT FOR CLASS #7

1. Circle the following according to how important they are to you: 1= very important, 2 = pretty important, 3 = not important at all.

   Your best friend should be equal to you in

	Very Imp.	Pretty Imp.	Not Imp.
Height (how tall you both are)	1	2	3
Weight (how heavy you both are)	1	2	3
Intelligence (how smart you both are)	1	2	3
Strength (how strong you both are)	1	2	3
Same Sex (both boys or both girls)	1	2	3
Background (families and houses similar)	1	2	3
Music (you like the same music)	1	2	3
Activities (you like to do the same things)	1	2	3
Language (you both speak the same language)	1	2	3
Age (you are both the same age)	1	2	3

2. Choose from the list above the *most* important way you should be equal with your best friend.

ACTIVITIES FOR CLASS #7

1. Ask the students to sit in a circle. Pass out the handout. Ask them to answer question #1 on their own.

2. Break into groups of 4-5 and ask them to answer question #2 and share their response with each other. Give them some time to discuss the issue after all have shared their answer.

3. Bring the students back to the large group. Be sure to give them the opportunity to report on their work in the small groups. Read the story to them, asking them to read along silently. Begin by asking the whole group how important it is to them that they see their friends as equals. After some discussion, ask them to answer the question asked at the very end of the story.

(These times are approximate only)

1. Form circle; answer question #1	5 mins.
2. Small group; answer #2 and discuss	15 mins.
3. Small-group reports; Read the story and discuss	20 mins.
	40 mins.

Class #8   *Pandora's Box,*
                          A Tale from Greece

Summary/Purpose:

One of the great mythic tales is the story of Pandora's box. It is a story about wanting to know something which is hidden from us, about curiosity and the consequences that can ensue when we allow it to consume us. We, your students, and indeed every human being we know are in one respect just like Pandora. As a species, we are intensely curious. We love to find out new things, new pieces of information. This desire takes the most various forms. For some, it is scientific and scholarly investigation; for others, it is watching or reading news reports. Still others exercise their curiosity through travel, and almost all of us spend time gossiping. From our earliest years, everyone talks about other people they know. Sometimes we do this to get information we need; at other times we do it simply because we are curious. In fact we can see this aspect of ourselves and how similar we are to Pandora when we remember that almost nothing stirs our interest like being told that a piece of information is being intentionally hidden from us, that it is a secret.

It is rarely our task as teachers to develop or instill curiosity in our students. Rather our task is the very difficult one of directing their natural curiosity into areas or subjects that are educationally appropriate. Sometimes the problem we face is that subject matters seem too alien to students' daily interests to engage their already existing curiosity. At other times our students already believe they know an answer and become complacent. Still other students may fear the risk of learning something new. Each of these situations poses special problems for us; each of us has different solutions. However, we will not be able to serve this function for our students whenever they need it, for there is simply not enough time. Nor will we be able to go with them as a constant guide throughout their lives. We must therefore find strategies to enable them to accomplish this task for themselves. Touchstones discussions are an environment where students learn both to direct their own curiosity and, through that, to begin to teach themselves.

One of the first steps in this process is to give students practice in using their own experience and interests to become engaged with a text or a subject matter. Up to now, Touchpebbles texts have been used to provoke students to reflect on the multiple perspectives their experience offers them. In today's lesson, your task and theirs is to use their experience of curiosity to explore why Pandora did what she did. In the class the students will be asked to report from their experience an incident which is similar to that in the myth. They are to elaborate on a situation that happened to them or someone they know where unrestrained curiosity caused problems. Of course none of them has ever been in the exact situation described in the story. However, all of them will have experienced various aspects of curiosity.

The handout will assist them in attending to this topic. It begins by having them rank subjects, people, or types of events they are curious about. In short, what most provokes their curiosity? In small groups, they are to help one another explain why their curiosity takes certain directions and not others. After they have explored the general issue of curiosity, read the story to them. You should begin the discussion by asking them why Pandora's curiosity increased because she was forbidden to open the box. As they begin to investigate this question, invite them to recount comparable cases from their own experience. For example, ask them why being told that something was none of their business made them even more eager to know it.

Pandora's Box   (Student vol., p. 23)
A Tale from Greece

Zeus, most powerful of all the Greek gods, was still angry that the giant Prometheus had given the gift of fire to mankind. He was also angry with humans because of the new skills they developed with the help of the fire. So Zeus thought up a dreadful plan to get even. He created the first woman, who was to be given to Prometheus' brother, another giant whose name was Epimetheus. This first woman was made from clay on the mountain of Olympus, and she was very beautiful. All the gods and goddesses gave her something to make her even more perfect. One taught her to sing, another gave her the gift of speaking well, and yet another gave her the skill of getting along with others. Finally, Zeus gave her a beautiful golden box, but he told her that she must never open it. Then he sent her to earth to be the wife of Epimetheus.

Epimetheus loved her as soon as he saw her and forgot that his brother had warned him never to accept a gift from Zeus. He asked the woman, whose name was Pandora, about the box, and she told him that she had been ordered never to open it. But she felt sure it contained something valuable and wonderful. "Let us open it together," she said to her husband. Epimetheus, however, also told her never to open it, for he feared what Zeus might have done.

But the more Pandora was told not to open it, the more she wondered about what was inside. She fought against the temptation for a long time. Then, one day, she gave in, and said to herself, "If I just open it up a tiny bit, peep inside to see, and then close it quickly, no one will ever know except me."

She opened it just a little, but out rushed a dark cloud of ugly, buzzing insects which swarmed in all directions. There was no way Pandora could ever get them back inside. The great number of insects that spread all over the earth became the spirits of hatred, greed, pain, illness, and war, all the evils that have hurt mankind ever since.

But one last gift remained in the box. It was the spirit of *Hope*. Pandora wondered whether that might be any use against all the evils she had let loose.

HANDOUT FOR CLASS #8

1. Do you get more curious when someone tells you not to be?   ☐ Yes   ☐ No

2. We are all curious about different things. Circle the number below that best describes how curious these situations make you feel.

	very curious	a bit curious	don't care
a. I know my parents have hidden presents for me in the house.	1	2	3
b. My friend won't tell me a secret.	1	2	3
c. Someone I don't like won't tell me who is spreading a bad rumor about me.	1	2	3
d. My teacher shows me a book she thinks I should read.	1	2	3
e. I wonder how lost dogs find their way home.	1	2	3
f. I visit some place I've never been to before, and someone asks me if I'd like to explore it.	1	2	3

3. Think of a story where too much curiosity led to trouble.

ACTIVITIES FOR CLASS #8

1. Ask the students to sit in a circle. Pass out the handout and ask them to fill out answers to questions #1 and #2. Ask them to think of a story they could volunteer for question #3.

2. Break them into small groups (4-5) and have them discuss what things from the list in question #2 they are very curious about. Ask them to decide whether it is true that the more someone tells them not to be curious, the more curious they get.

3. Gather them back into a large circle and read the story to them, asking them to read it silently. Ask them why Pandora's curiosity increased because she was forbidden to open the box.

4. For the last 10 minutes or so of class, invite them to share anecdotes that show how too much curiosity led to problems.

(These times are approximate only)

1. Sit in circle; answer questions #1 and #2	10 mins.
2. Small-group work	10 mins.
3. Read story to large group; discuss	10 mins.
4. Ask volunteers to share stories of curiosity	<u>10 mins.</u>
	40 mins.

Class #9   *The Confessions,*
                         by St. Augustine of Hippo

Summary/Purpose:

In the last meeting your students considered why we enjoy learning secrets, why our natural curiosity increases when we are told that something is none of our business. Curiosity is a kind of thinking that leads to knowing and understanding. However, we not only think, we also do things. A comparable case about our actions comes up in this week's class. We are all familiar with how tempting it is to do something which is forbidden. The moment we are told we are not to do something, that forbidden action takes on a new and sometimes irresistible force.

In this week's reading, St. Augustine recounts an incident from his youth when he and some friends stole pears. In the story he tells us both that he knew stealing was wrong and that he didn't even want what he stole. Yet, in spite of that he derived pleasure from stealing. He enjoyed it precisely because it was forbidden.

This is a topic with which all of your students have had a great deal of experience. Though few of them have probably ever stolen anything, they have all disobeyed various people in positions of authority, their parents and other relatives, their previous teachers and probably you too, and even the ground rules which they should follow in Touchstones. In other words, at one level they know as much about this unusual feeling as Augustine or any of us. On this topic, they are therefore experts and each student will have something to offer. This is important for you to realize because it is likely that some of your students have not spoken in the large-group discussion yet or have only participated in very small ways. Today's session is therefore an opportunity to increase the number of participants in the discussion.

It is not crucial that all students speak in every discussion. In fact, that is unlikely or even impossible. What is important is that everyone is a potential speaker. In other words, what is important is that not the same people are always silent or always speaking. That has probably occurred to a certain extent in your class, and you will need to make an effort to modify it. Today's text is a useful tool to accomplish that goal. It often happens that some of the students who don't speak are acting that way because they still view Touchstones discussions as a required school activity and thus are as hostile to it as to regular classes. Such students are behaving in a way not entirely dissimilar to Augustine. You should realize that these students probably know more about the type of situation Augustine describes than those students who generally speak in class and who do not feel tempted to resist authority.

The handout will help you bring the two different groups of students into the discussion. The first question asks for reasons that people would have for not stealing. This question will be the kind to which your "good" students generally volunteer answers. The second question is more difficult since it involves acknowledging one's temptations. However, we have found that many students who don't freely participate in organized class activities are the ones who are more forward in answering this question. You should therefore encourage, even by asking them directly, what responses they gave. You should view this text as an occasion for increasing the number of participants in the discussion.

The Confessions, (Student vol., p. 25)
by St. Augustine of Hippo

No thief, not even a rich one, will let another man, even one who is very poor, steal from him. This shows that everyone knows in their heart that stealing is wrong. Yet I both wanted to steal and did steal. And what is so surprising, I was not made to do it because I needed anything. I stole something which I already had. I stole pears, though I already had pears which were better than the ones I took. I had no wish to eat what I stole. What I enjoyed was stealing itself.

Near my parents' garden was a neighbor's pear tree. Though it was loaded with pears, they looked rotten. Even so, some friends and I got the idea of shaking the pears off the tree and carrying them away. We set out late at night and stole all the fruit we could carry. We tasted a few and then threw the rest to the pigs. We took no pleasure in eating the pears, nor in being out late at night. What we liked was simply doing something which was forbidden.

HANDOUT FOR CLASS #9

1. We have all felt tempted to take something that belongs to someone else. Probably, you have not done it: that is, you resisted the temptation to take something. Try to remember that feeling of *wanting* to take something, and also the feeling of *resisting*, of *not* actually taking it. Which of the following seems most true? (check most true) Which is least true? (check least true) Read them all before you make your decision and **pick only two.**

I do not steal because	most true	least true
a. I know it's wrong.	☐	☐
b. someone might see me.	☐	☐
c. other people will not like me.	☐	☐
d. I might get punished.	☐	☐
e. I don't want other people to steal from me.	☐	☐
f. it's against the law.	☐	☐

2. If something is wrong (like taking something that belongs to someone else) and people are told not to do it, why do some people feel very strongly that they want to do it anyway? Circle the letters of those that seem true to you.

   a. When people see something they want, they feel like taking it.
   b. It's exciting to do things that are wrong.
   c. The more people are told not to do something, the more they want to do it.
   d. It makes people feel smart to get away with it.
   e. Their friends make them want to do it.

ACTIVITIES FOR CLASS #9

1. Ask the students to sit in a circle. Pass out the handouts. Ask them to fill out answers for questions #1 and #2. Since the handouts are rather long, you may wish to read the questions aloud and answer any questions they may have about the instructions. Give students about 8 minutes for this.

2. Ask your students to volunteer their answers for either question #1 or #2. When students stop volunteering, begin asking students directly what their responses were. Every student should provide an answer for either question.

3. Read the text aloud and have students read silently. Point out that Augustine says he stole the pears because he was "simply doing something which was forbidden." Ask them if that seems true to them and what he means by that. At some point, you might ask them which of the reasons given in question #2 might be closest to Augustine's reason and why.

(These times are approximate only)

1. Sit in circle	2 mins.
2. Answer questions #1 and #2	8 mins.
3. Student volunteer responses to #1 or #2	10 mins.
4. Read story	2 mins.
5. Discussion	<u>18 mins.</u>
	40 mins.

Class #10   *Emile* or *On Education*,
                      by Jean-Jacques Rousseau

Summary/Purpose:

Past classes have explored perspectives of many kinds. In some cases, students compared different perspectives of the same object. In other cases, how students saw themselves was matched against how others saw them. Probably, the students had some previous experience of these differences. In this week's class, the task will move to a higher level. The students will be asked *to take on* or *imagine* a perspective. In other words, they will have to imagine how something would appear to them if they were different than they are now.

Because taking on a perspective is one of the crucial skills which must be learned in order to teach oneself, it will be practiced throughout the rest of the year. In order to grasp another's point of view adequately, and in particular to understand one's own opinions fully, taking on or imagining a perspective is decisive. This is because we frequently hear what others say inaccurately, that is we hear what we want to hear or what we expect to hear. In addition, we rarely realize that some of our own opinions are not objectively correct but rather are a legitimate but nonetheless one-sided slant on events, issues, or people. Because we are, in a sense, so close to ourselves, we make others much more similar to ourselves than they really are. We must therefore make the effort to see ourselves more clearly. This clarity will make it possible both to understand others and to evaluate our own beliefs, needs, and goals. The text by Rousseau and the handout will encourage your students to imagine or create a vantage point from which to view themselves.

Rousseau's text is about how children should be raised. It focuses on a danger every parent acknowledges: spoiling a child. Children are born helpless and dependent. From the very start of their lives, we take care of them. When they cry or ask for something, our inclination as parents is to figure out what they need and supply it. Every parent who responds to a small child is cast into this situation. Both child and parent develop a definite pattern of behavior, habit, and expectation. Rousseau's text focuses on how dangerous it is to allow this early relationship to continue. The danger, he states, is raising a child who is spoiled. In one sense it appears easier not to change definite ways of behaving, for us and for a child. In many ways it seems easier to continue to try to supply whatever a child calls for. However, Rousseau points out that at some point we will have to say "No." The moment we choose to say "No" is crucial. If we wait too long, the child will become a tyrant who expects everything and becomes furious when we eventually have to refuse. This is the spoiled child. Rousseau takes this familiar situation one step further. He looks at what will occur to such a child when he or she enters the larger world, for example, school. Other adults or other children react very differently from a child's parents. The result for the spoiled child is a great shock. The child becomes uncertain and afraid and feels very weak.

Many students in your class are still living through this transition from life at home to life at school. Some, in fact, are spoiled children who may be experiencing just what Rousseau describes. Even if they aren't, they have heard that warning or accusation often enough. They therefore will have very definite ideas about spoiled children though probably none will see themselves that way. The handout asks them to list some of the characteristics of a spoiled child. This question will implicitly make them look at themselves. They are then asked to imagine themselves as raising a child and to decide how they would treat the child in order to avoid spoiling it. They are really being asked how they should have been and should now be treated. It encourages them to *take on* a perspective on themselves. They must look at themselves not merely as their peers view them but as adults, parents, and teachers might view them. This is a crucial step of imagination because they have not had the experience of being an adult.

Emile or *On Education,* (Student vol., p. 27)
by Jean-Jacques Rousseau

Do you know the most likely way to make your children unhappy? You can make them unhappy by giving them everything they want. When it is so easy for them to get what they want, they want more and more things. They will want your hat, your watch, and even the birds in the air. So sooner or later, because you can't keep up with them, you will have to say "No." This will cause more pain than if you had not tried to give them everything they had wanted. Such children believe they own the world. They think all people are their slaves. When you try to explain why you finally said "No," they think it's just an excuse. They feel they have been wronged and hurt by you. They begin to hate everyone. They are never grateful. They never thank anyone.

    Could such a child ever be happy? No. They are tyrants. I have seen children raised this way fill the air with their cries the moment they are not obeyed. They complain all the time. They beat on the table. And what are they like when they grow up and go out into the world or start school? There, they are surprised when they don't get their own way. In the world, people don't jump to get them what they want. They thought everything was theirs, and now they can't understand what has happened. They become afraid and mixed up and begin to feel they are very weak. When they were younger, they felt they could do anything. Now, they feel they can do nothing. Nature has made children to be loved and helped. But should we fear and obey them?

HANDOUT FOR CLASS #10

1. You probably know a spoiled child. You may have called someone spoiled. *All* the sentences below are true to some extent, but some are truer than others. Circle the number of the one sentence that you think is the most true.

    1. A spoiled child expects others always to do what he wants.
    2. A spoiled child never considers other people's feelings.
    3. A spoiled child makes life miserable for everyone nearby.
    4. A spoiled child is selfish.
    5. A spoiled child never does what you ask.
    6. A spoiled child is never satisfied.

2. What is the best way to avoid spoiling someone? Circle the number of the sentence that is most true or write your own answer.

    1. You should punish them.
    2. You should feel sorry for them.
    3. You should ignore them.
    4. You should try to change their mind by talking to them.
    5. You should take away privileges or things they like.
    6. Other (your own idea).

ACTIVITIES FOR CLASS #10

1. Ask the students to sit in a circle. Ask them what people mean when they say someone is spoiled. Ask for a volunteer to give an answer and from that student go around the circle until all the students have given an answer. Write down the list of answers on the blackboard. Allow the students to discuss their different answers and then ask them to help you make another list of things that spoiled children ask for most.

2. Read the text and have the students read it silently. Pass out the handout and break the students into small groups (4-5) and have them first think of individual answers to questions #1 and #2. Encourage the small groups to agree about the best way to avoid spoiling a child.

3. Reconvene the large circle and have each small group report its consensus on the best way to treat someone so they don't become spoiled. Let the group discuss the different answers but be sure each group reports.

(These times are approximate only)

1. Sit in circle	1 mins.
2. Definition of "spoiled"	9 mins.
3. Read text	3 mins.
4. Small groups; answer and discuss questions #1 and #2	6 mins.
5. Small-group reports and discussion	21 mins.
	40 mins.

Class #11   *The Pillow,*
A Tale from the Middle East

Summary/Purpose:

One of the goals of Touchstones is for students to learn how to teach and learn from others. This, as we teachers know all too well, is never a simple or straightforward task. Parents often imagine, and your students will too, that teaching is a kind of one-directional activity. The teacher knows something or has a piece of information, and the task is simply to place this information in the mind of the student, like moving a table from one room to another. Of course, stating the situation in such bald terms makes us immediately realize how inaccurate this characterization is. Teaching, even at the very simplest levels, is a highly complex activity in which both student and teacher must cooperate. The student must have a fairly accurate sense of what he or she needs to know and, of course, a desire to satisfy that need. The teacher must also recognize what the student needs to learn and also what the student knows in order to develop a strategy to make a bridge from the familiar to what is unknown. Your students can explore these relations this week in the simple, familiar form of giving advice.

Giving advice is a type of teaching which all of your students have experienced. They have all certainly received advice and probably most or all have at one time or other attempted to give it. It is useful to view teaching through the model of giving advice because it is clear that the activity crucially involves both people. While giving advice sometimes succeeds, more frequently it fails. The reasons for its failure bring out the issues involved in all teaching. Sometimes giving advice fails because a person doesn't realize he or she needs advice; it becomes a difficult and often insurmountable task to get that across. However, even if someone recognizes that they need advice, they can still resist. Sometimes people will only accept advice when they ask for it and then only from particular people. If advice is offered without being asked for, it is frequently refused. It would be useful to have the group discuss why. And yet sometimes even when it is asked for from a particular person, the advice is still not taken. This can occur because the advisor does not know how to present the advice so that it makes sense to the other person's perspective. These issues will be brought up in the handout and the text.

The story is about two men who meet at an inn. The younger man begins to complain about his life, that he is poor and must work long hours, and the older man tries unsuccessfully to get him to stop complaining. He therefore gives the young man a magic pillow. While the young man sleeps, he dreams that he has been given what he has been asking for, wealth, power, and position, but also that possessing what he has wished for has put his life in jeopardy. The dream is so vivid that he feels it is really happening. This makes him change his mind. Thus, the dream proves to be a successful piece of advice. The question which arises is how could the old man have accomplished what the dream was able to achieve.

The handout brings up the same issue by making the students take on both perspectives, as advisees and as advisors. Other issues that the story raises are whether the difference in age prevents the young man from accepting the old man's advice and whether the young man knows that the old man spoke into the pillow so as to influence the dream. This seems possible because the young man thanks the old man for the pillow and the advice. The successful strategy in the story seems to be to help advisees accept advice by making them feel the consequences of what they plan on doing. This tactic acknowledges that people tend not to accept advice that contradicts what they want. You might encourage the students to suggest and explore different strategies for giving advice. Two possible strategies are (a) raising cases of people in similar situations who have come to regret acting as they once wished and (b) listening hard and trying to decide what someone really wants and explain how one does or doesn't achieve it. There are, of course, other routes which your students might suggest.

The Pillow,   **(Student vol., p. 29)**
A Tale from the Middle East

An old wise man stopped at an inn for the night. He was dressed simply and carried one bag in which were some books and a few clothes. Soon, a young farm worker came in wearing ragged clothes and sat beside the wise man. They began talking and telling each other stories and laughing. But then the young man started grumbling and saying how poor he was. He became sad telling how he was always hungry and unhappy and had no hope of making his life better.

"You look healthy and strong to me," said the old man. "Why complain now after you were laughing and content just five minutes ago?"

"I have to work hard from sunrise to sundown," said the young farm worker. "I should be a great general or a wealthy businessman or a popular singer. That way people would see how important I am."

When they were both tired and were ready for bed and sleep, the wise man offered the youngster a pillow and said, "This is a special pillow that will grant all your wishes if you sleep on it." It was a strange pillow, for it was made of blue glass and was hollow inside and open at both ends. The young man eagerly took it and laid himself down and went to sleep. In no time at all the following things happened to him. He married a beautiful girl, he made a lot of money, he bought more and more land, and he made more money. He became so important that he was appointed Chief Adviser to the King. Then one day, a crafty assistant of the king accused him of stealing from the king and then lying about it. He pleaded that he was innocent, but the king sentenced him to die. Just as the sword was raised to cut off his head, he woke up. He was still at the inn. The wise man was lying beside him with his head by one end of the magic pillow. The innkeeper was cooking breakfast.

The young man was still shaking at breakfast and ate his food without speaking. When he had finished, he went to the wise man and kneeled humbly before him and said, "Thank you for the pillow, sir, and for the lesson you taught me. Now I know better how I should live well!"

HANDOUT FOR CLASS #11

1. Why do *you* sometimes not listen to someone who is trying to help you decide what to do? Check TWO of the following possibilities:

    - ☐ You're too sure you are right.
    - ☐ You want what you want too much.
    - ☐ You don't like people telling you what to do.
    - ☐ You only listen to one or two very close friends your own age.
    - ☐ You only listen to older people.
    - ☐ You don't like to admit you're wrong.
    - ☐ (your own reason)

2. It's hard to accept even very good advice, especially if we want to do the opposite. Suppose your friend is angry with someone and wants to get back. You believe it's wrong, but your friend is too mad to listen. How would you get your friend to listen?

    - ☐ Keep repeating your opinion.
    - ☐ Tell a story about the bad things that happened to someone else who did as your friend plans to do.
    - ☐ Tell your friend you won't *be* their friend if they don't listen to you.
    - ☐ Take your friend to three or four more people who agree with you.
    - ☐ Talk with your friend until they calm down.
    - ☐ (Your own suggestion)

ACTIVITIES FOR CLASS #11

1. Ask your students to sit in a circle. Pass out the handout. Ask them to answer questions #1 and #2 individually. Help them by reading the questions aloud and answering any questions. You may have to explain the word "advice" to them.

2. Form small groups of 4-5 and ask them to share with each other their answers to question #1. With their own preferences in mind, have them discuss which strategy in question #2 will work the best to overcome the kinds of resistance they have expressed in answering question #1. Encourage the small groups to agree on a strategy and to provide reasons why that strategy would be best.

3. After 10 minutes, have them return to the large circle and have the small groups report.

4. Read the story, having them read it silently. Ask them why the young man wouldn't take the old man's advice to begin with and why he changes his mind. At some point, you may point out to them that the old man probably talks into the hollow glass pillow to influence the young man. Why then isn't the young man angry at being fooled? Does the young man know the old man is talking into the pillow?

(These time are approximate only)

1. Sit in circle	1 min.
2. Answer questions #1 and #2	5 mins.
3. Small-group strategies	10 mins.
4. Form large group; small-group reports	6 mins.
5. Read story and discuss	<u>18 mins.</u>
	40 mins.

Class #12 *Catching Fish in the Forest,*
A Tale from Russia

Summary/Purpose:

We all depend on others for various kinds of assistance in our daily lives. Nowhere is this more conspicuous than in our need for information. Since none of us can know everything, each of us must find ways to uncover the information we need, and all of us must learn to evaluate and assess the continuous barrage of facts that pour in on us from friends, adults, and the media. A very astute grammar school teacher once said, "The truly intelligent person is not one who knows everything but who knows where to go to find out. That's what we should be teaching." One place where students can begin to learn how to do this is in Touchstones discussions. For students generally receive information from two directions, neither of which readily permits serious assessment of what is told. The formal route is from teachers. Teachers are believed because they are generally trusted, not because students have evaluated the evidence for what we tell them. The second is from informal sources outside school and from other learning situations. Information from these sources is either believed or not depending on the attitude of the children involved, and not because they have assessed what they have heard. Both of these sources of learning are essential, but it is equally essential that our students learn to evaluate evidence and think for themselves. They can learn this in Touchstones discussions because this situation occupies an intermediate position. It is a formal learning situation, but one in which all contributors are roughly equal. Because there is neither an authority nor an expert present nor ties of friendship connecting the students, they come to expect evidence for what people say.

Typically we use certain criteria to assess evidence. For example, in the early 17th century, René Descartes suggested that we should doubt everything we hear or read, and undertake to prove it to ourselves before we believe it. Fortunately Descartes is probably the only person ever to have tried this. Our general attitude is that we believe what we hear unless we have some reason to doubt it. In normal cases, our reasons for doubt can be of two sorts. Either we doubt the person who supplies the information, even if what he tells us is quite ordinary and unsurprising, or we trust the informant, even if what he tells us does not easily fit with all the other information we have previously accepted. However, in either situation we may ultimately decide on the basis of evidence to accept the piece of information. The handout and text will focus the students on these issues of evidence.

The handout has the students look at a report of a very unusual event from two perspectives. In the first case, they saw something with their own eyes but no one believes them. They are asked to select how they would respond. In the second case, a friend tells them something which they find unbelievable and they must choose a response. In discussion you might have them consider the weight they would attach to the same report told by different people: a parent, a sibling, a friend, or a stranger.

The story unites the two issues. A farmer who finds some treasure knows his wife will tell everyone about it. He therefore decides to influence how people will take what she says. This is the strategy lawyers employ when they diminish the credibility of a hostile witness. In the story, the farmer creates a fantastic or unbelievable situation which he then has his wife observe. When she accurately reports what she has seen, everyone is so surprised by what she claims (namely, that it rained cookies and a rabbit was caught in a river) that they believe her husband when he tells everyone that she is crazy. Even though she tells the truth, what she sees so disagrees with everyone's experience that they conclude something is wrong with her. You might invite the students to bring up cases where they were surprised at a piece of information but later came to believe it. They should discuss why they changed their minds.

Catching Fish in the Forest, (Student vol., p. 31)
A Tale from Russia

One day, a farm worker was digging in a field and found a large box of treasure. He took it home and said to his wife, "Look what I found. Where can we hide it?" They decided to bury it in the dirt floor. But then the man thought to himself, "My wife can't keep secrets. Soon the whole village will know about the treasure box." So he dug it up and buried it again behind the chicken coop. Then he went out and bought some oatmeal cookies, some fish, and he caught and killed a rabbit.

Very early next morning, he quietly went out of their hut, and left the fish on different paths in the forest. He threw the cookies up into the trees, and he tied the dead rabbit to a line which he dropped into the river. Later that morning he said to his wife, "Please come with me into the forest and help me catch fish on the footpath for our dinner tonight."

She was amazed and cried out, "Fish in the forest?"

"Yes," he said. "I'm told there are several biting there today." So they went into the forest.

Very soon, she found a codfish on the footpath, then other small fish nearby. She couldn't believe her eyes, but she picked them up and put them in her basket. She looked up, and there on an oak tree's branches she saw some cookies, and over there some more cookies in a maple tree, and yet more in an elm tree. She showed her husband, and he said, "I must look to see if I caught a rabbit in my trap." So he pulled the fishing line from the river, and there was the dead rabbit. "This is unbelievable!" she cried. But she added the rabbit to the fish and cookies in her basket, and when they returned home, she cooked a fine meal.

A week later, the man was told to come to the duke's palace. He knew the secret of his buried treasure had been told to people by his wife and that the duke had heard about it. Sure enough, the duke asked him, "Did you find some treasure and bury it in your house?" "No," replied the man. The duke said, "But your wife has been telling everyone that you did." "Oh, she's crazy," said the man. "She sees things that are not there. Just a few days ago she told me she had caught fish in the forest, a rabbit in the river, and found cookies in the trees."

So the duke called for the wife and asked her whether her story about the treasure was true and when it had happened. "Of course it's true," she said. "It happened the day before I caught fish in the forest; in fact, the night before that, it had rained cookies. My husband caught a rabbit in the river with a fishing line the same day, too."

Now the duke knew the woman was crazy, and the man kept the treasure he had found.

HANDOUT FOR CLASS #12

1. You have seen something with your own eyes that is amazing. When you tell your friends, they think you're making it up. How do you react when they won't believe you? Check **ONE.**

    ☐ Tell the story again.
    ☐ Try to think of similar things they have seen and believed.
    ☐ Explain what you saw in more and more detail.
    ☐ Quietly walk away.
    ☐ Ask them to trust you.
    ☐ (Write some other reaction here)

2. A friend tells you something you just can't believe. They tell you they're not fooling you, that it's really true, and that you must trust them. Yet it is still too hard to believe. What do you do? Check **ONE**.

    ☐ Ask for more details to see if your friend changes any part of the story.
    ☐ Keep trying to get them to admit they are making it up.
    ☐ Ask other people you trust what they think and agree with whatever they say.
    ☐ Believe your friend even though it's unbelievable.
    ☐ Refuse to talk about it anymore and continue to believe it's not true.
    ☐ (Write some other reaction here)

ACTIVITIES FOR CLASS #12

1. Ask the students sit in a circle. Pass out the handout and ask them to answer both questions.

2. Divide the class into small groups and have them discuss their responses. Ask them whose account of something amazing they would most readily believe: a parent's, a brother's or sister's, a friend's, or a stranger's, and why. It may help if students can relate stories of not believing something and then changing their minds. What changed their minds?

3. Call all the students back into the circle and read the story, having them read it silently. Ask them why the duke didn't believe the wife, even though she told the truth, and whether she could have done anything to convince him. Ask the groups to share any stories they came up with where people were initially surprised but later came to believe something unusual. Why would the townspeople believe the woman when she tells them that she and her husband have found hidden treasure, but not when she reports that cookies were in the trees?

(These times are approximate only)

1. Sit in circle	1 min.
2. Answer handout questions	4 mins.
3. Small-group work	12 mins.
4. Read story	3 mins.
5. Discussion and small-group anecdotes	<u>20 mins.</u>
	40 mins.

Class #13 *The Eagle,*
A Poem by Alfred, Lord Tennyson

Summary/Purpose:

Language serves many different purposes. We can use it to meet the needs of different audiences, to describe a situation clearly, or to make that situation more or less dramatic. All of these uses have definite advantages and disadvantages, some, however, with disadvantages so pronounced that we find it difficult to see any advantage. It is very important for a discussion class, which operates through language, to explore these issues. In this week's class the students will start this exploration. The class will consider three short accounts of the same event, the flight of an eagle. One of these accounts is a poem by Tennyson, the other two are short prose descriptions. The class will consider the advantages and disadvantages of each version.

In looking at this poem, students will see that it takes an unremarkable event, an eagle flying off a cliff (expressed clearly in version #2) and uses language to create other images whose purpose seems to be to convey a dynamic sense of what one might call the eagle's nature. The poem may be the most dramatic version and present several arresting images, but it will seem inaccessible to most of your students, both for its vocabulary ("azure world") and the images it presents. What does it mean, for example, to say that an eagle has "crooked hands?"

The poem describes an eagle sitting high up in a clear blue sky, clutching a rocky cliff edge. The eagle perches so high up that the presumably large sea waves below look like wrinkles. Then the eagle suddenly plunges down from its perch, "like a thunderbolt." Version #1 preserves the dramatic tone of the poem but clarifies the scene by translating some of the words and simplifying the images. The poem, for example, never calls its subject an eagle (except in the title) and indeed provides some images, like "crooked hands," that make one think of a human rather than a bird. Version #2 is the least dramatic and tries to tell clearly and plainly what the scene is. It is like a movie of the scene.

You will need to provide a great deal of guidance and even direct help in order for discussion to take place. The handout is set up to ask students first to draw what is described by version #2 so that they can begin with a clear picture. Feel free to define words or clarify images as you see fit, but let your explanations be brief and to the point. Students will benefit from struggling to understand the poem and from beginning to appreciate the variety of uses one can make of language. Students compare versions #1 and #2 before you read the poem to them. Once you read the poem, students concentrate on listing what is new about it and what a drawing of the poem might look like. How would their original drawings have to be changed? The discussion will hinge on what they prefer about each account of the event, and why.

In the discussion you might encourage them to indicate their preference for one of the versions and to give a reason. Probably most students will prefer version #2, which is short and clear. You might ask them whether there is anything from version #1 or the poem that they feel is important yet not present in version #2. How would they change version #2 to include what they feel is missing? In the poem the words in the two stanzas end in rhymes. In the first stanza the final words are "hands," "lands," and "stands;" in the second they are "crawls," "walls," and "falls." You might ask them if that adds anything important to their sense of what is happening.

This class will be quite different from others you have had. As must be clear from the summary, you will need to be much more present as a teacher than you usually are both in answering questions and making suggestions. Your class has now had quite a bit of experience of discussions which are principally intended to develop skills. This week's class will enable all of you to see to what extent discussions can help in exploring content. This will involve you and them in changing roles during the class. They will need to use discussion to figure out what information they need from you and then use that information to further their own discussion. Later in the year, you will attempt this difficult task again and be able to gauge their improvement.

The Eagle, (Student vol., p. 35)
A Poem by Alfred, Lord Tennyson

1. High up in the sky, the lone eagle grips an edge of the rocky cliff with his claws. The bright sun shines down from a clear blue sky. He gazes down on the sea below, which is lightly ruffled by the wind. Suddenly, he swoops down.

2. The eagle stands by himself on the top of the cliff high up in the sky. The sun shines in the blue sky. He looks at the sea waves below and flies down.

The Eagle,
    by Alfred, Lord Tennyson

He clasps the crag with crooked hands;
Close to the sun in lonely lands,
Ringed with the azure world, he stands.

The wrinkled sea beneath him crawls;
He watches from his mountain walls,
And like a thunderbolt he falls.

HANDOUT FOR CLASS #13

1. Draw what you think is being described in version #2. Use the back of the handout.

2. Versions #1 and #2 have many differences. Two differences are listed below. Make a ✓ for the one you prefer.

   a. Do you prefer

           the lone eagle... ☐, or

           The eagle stands by himself ☐?

   b. Do you prefer

           He gazes down... ☐, or

           He looks at... ☐?

3. Write one more difference you can find between version #1 and version #2.

   From #1.

   From #2.

ACTIVITIES FOR CLASS #13

1. Ask your students to sit in a circle and read the two prose paragraphs several times. Ask the students to read along silently and to ask any questions they may have about the words.

2. Pass out the handout and ask them to draw the scene described by prose version #2. Have the students share their drawings, remarking on any differences in the scene. That is, they should look for differences in *what* they have drawn but not criticize *how* other students have drawn it. If the class can agree on one or two drawings that seem to represent all the elements of the scene best, hang them where they can be seen.

3. Have the students answer questions #2 and #3. Then read the poem at least twice, having the students read it silently. Try to emphasize the rhyme scheme.

4. Break the class into small groups of 4-5 and have them discuss what new things the poem adds. Have them make a list (one student should volunteer to compile the list) of words they don't understand and of what they prefer about each version.

5. Call the students back into the large group and have the small groups report on their preferences. Ask them how they would change the drawings to match the way the poem now describes the scene.

(These times are approximate only)

1. Sit in circle	1 min.
2. Read versions #1 and #2 several times	4 mins.
3. Draw scene in #2	5 mins.
4. Judge drawings	8 mins.
5. Read poem; complete handout	3 mins.
6. Small-group list	6 mins.
7. Discussion	<u>13 mins.</u>
	40 mins.

Class #14   *They Share the Work,*
                              A Tale from Latvia

Summary/Purpose:

It is not uncommon for us to say things we don't mean. When we say to someone at dinner, "Can you pass the salt?", only a boor would reply, "Yes, I *can*" and do nothing. For we all recognize that the question wasn't asking whether we were *able* to pass the salt, even though that's what the question expressed. Instead, the questioner wanted the other person to pass the salt. Conversely, when someone says, "If you do that, I'll never speak to you again," we know in general they don't quite mean that.

When this distinction between words and their meanings occurs in commands or laws, it is often called a distinction between the spirit and the letter of the law. Just as lawyers and their clients use, and sometimes abuse, this distinction, so too do children when they want to "get around" some parental rule that they find personally restrictive. For example, they may cleverly obey exactly what their parents *said*, while clearly violating their *intention*.

The text for today's lesson contains interesting echoes of this theme. In the text, an industrious man sows a field with wheat and uses the grain to make flour for bread. A lazy man sees this and makes a deal with the first man for half of next year's crop. The lazy man agrees to collect everything that grows above ground. The worker decides to plant potatoes. The result is that the worker gets all the food, while the lazy man comes away with the worthless part, the potato vines.

The story makes it perfectly clear that the lazy man was trying to trick the other into giving him "free" food; but it is not clear whether the industrious man chose to plant potatoes in order to outwit the lazy man. In any event, the lazy man did not get the deal he wanted because he asked the wrong question. He didn't say what he meant. He wanted the half of the crop which could be eaten. Instead, he asked for the top half of the crop, though it is not clear that the worker would have made a deal at all if the lazy man had said what he really wanted.

The handout for this week should be completed before reading the story. It specifically calls attention to the difference between what is actually said and what the speaker almost certainly intends. On the basis of a hypothetical instruction from a parent or guardian, the students must judge the appropriateness of three different actions. After they have judged the actions and discussed this in small groups, you should read the story to them. The question they should discuss as a whole class is whether either of the men was honest and truthful; that is, they should try to answer the last question of the story. If I can say, "I gave you exactly what you asked for," does that always make me honest?

They Share the Work,   (Student vol., p. 37)
A Tale from Latvia

Once there was a time when only two men lived in the world. One was good and honest, the other selfish and mean.

In the spring, one of them dug in a field and planted wheat. The other man watched him doing this and was very puzzled. He watched day after day. As summer came with its rain and sun, the grain grew tall above the ground. In the fall, the first man cut the ripe wheat and made it into flour. Then he baked bread. He used his plow to make the soil better by mixing the roots of the wheat into the earth.

Next year, the second man went to the first and said, "Let's work together and share the crop. I'll take the part above the soil. You have what's under the ground." The first man agreed, but this time he planted potatoes. In the fall, the first man kept the potatoes which were under the earth and had them to eat all winter. The second man had the worthless green tops which appear above the ground and was hungry all winter. He became angry and went to the first man to tell him he had been cheated. But the first man replied, "Why are you so angry with me? I gave you exactly what you asked for."

Which one of them was good and honest?

HANDOUT FOR CLASS #14

Your parent or guardian tells you to come home the shortest way. You understand that you're not supposed to play with your friends and get home late.

You could
1. come directly home by the shortest route, no playing; that's doing what your parent or guardian *meant*.

    If you did (1) would you be (check two if you want)
    obedient ( ), disobedient ( ), honest ( ), tricky ( )?

2. use the shortest way, but play with friends who live on that route and get home late; that is doing what your parent or guardian *said*.

    If you did (2) would you be (check two if you want)
    obedient ( ), disobedient ( ), honest ( ), tricky ( )?

3. use a longer route and take friends with you; but make sure you are home on time; coming home on time is doing what your parent or guardian *wants*.

    If you did (3) would you be (check two if you want)
    obedient ( ), disobedient ( ), honest ( ), tricky ( ),

ACTIVITIES FOR CLASS #14

1. Ask your students to sit in a circle. Pass out the handout sheet. Have them answer the three questions individually. Read the instructions to them and make sure that they understand what to do.

2. When they have finished filling out the sheet, break the class into small groups of 4-5 and ask them to discuss their answers with each other. Can they agree on the responses to any or all of the three? Do they have any stories to share of someone who obeyed the letter but not the spirit of someone's words?

3. Bring them back into the large circle and read the story. Ask them to answer the question in the last sentence of the story. You may wish to go around the circle and ask for volunteers to share their answers. You should answer too, but do not begin or end with yourself.

(These times are approximate only)

1. Sit in circle	1 mins.
2. Individual work on handout	9 mins.
3. Small-group discussion	12 mins.
4. Read story	4 mins.
5. Large-group discussion	<u>14 mins.</u>
	40 mins.

Class # 15   *TWO PORTRAITS:*
                   Portrait of a Clergyman,
                   by Albrecht Dürer
                   Marchesa Brigida Spinola Doria,
                   by Sir Peter Rubens

Summary/Purpose:

The common expression about not seeing the forest for the trees presents a new issue of perspective. We use that expression when we feel that someone is analyzing or viewing something so closely as to overlook the surroundings, the relations between the object analyzed or viewed and other objects around it. It is a typical complaint against our educational system that, even at its most successful, it turns out specialists who cannot appreciate the context within which their specialties fit or the relations their specialties have with others. On the other hand, we can also appreciate the expression that one misses the trees for the forest. This expression counterbalances the other. It implies that someone has concentrated on the context or the relations among objects without grasping the main object at the center of the relations. Such counterbalancing expressions imply that each approach misses an important aspect of a situation and that these two perspectives must be interconnected. One can neither appreciate the whole without studying the parts nor the parts without viewing the whole. The question is how to achieve both perspectives.

A common example will make the problem clearer. In an orchestra or a band, each member plays a specific instrument. That person must be skilled at playing that instrument as well as skilled at being able to mesh with the other instruments. To make this possible, a specific person often assists individuals in coordinating their playing with the other musicians. This person is the conductor in an orchestra or the bandleader in a band. In an orchestra, for example, the conductor's specific job is to know each part played by each instrument and also how these parts combine to form the whole piece of music. The conductor is the one person in the orchestra who must consider the whole. The members of the orchestra look to the conductor to enable them to unite their playing. A slightly different case is a bandleader who also plays an instrument. This person has a dual role as player and conductor. In this case the relation between knowing the part and knowing the whole is different. On the one hand, he is playing one part just like the other musicians and yet, like the conductor, he must also know the way all the parts fit together. In Touchstones discussions, your role so far has probably been that of an orchestra conductor. As the students become more skilled in the future (this has perhaps occasionally occurred already), you will be more like a bandleader. However, the ultimate goal in Touchstones discussions is neither of these cases. It is more like a group of musicians playing together where there is no specific leader. This often happens in jazz groups. Each performer in such groups must know what part to play and how it will fit into the whole created by the group. Similarly in Touchstones discussions, each student must eventually learn how simultaneously to be both participant and leader. This ability is one of the criteria for a true discussion and is also the kind of skill necessary for the political, social, and professional world our students must be prepared to enter. Increasingly in this highly technological and complex world, each person must develop concrete skills in a profession but also recognize how their skills interrelate with those of others. They must see both the trees and the forest.

    This week's lesson, handout, and text will help students begin to explore the relations of parts and wholes. For this we will use two portraits, one by Rubens, the other by Dürer. In the handout, students are asked to report on how they judge or assess someone they are meeting for the first time. Do they look at the eyes or skin as most revealing, or do they try to take more of the whole person into account by considering how people sit or generally how they hold themselves or the clothing they wear? The handout also allows them to suggest other factors such as a person's voice, how he or she speaks, a person's background, family, etc. The portraits raise the same question. The Dürer portrait focuses on a face, without much concern for where this person is or how he is dressed. The Rubens portrait is quite different. Though the Marchesa's face is quite important, it does not seem more important than how she stands, what she wears, or the room in which she stands. The Dürer portrait presents a person without a context. In the Rubens painting, the context is as important as the face. The students can decide that one is a more successful portrait or that each approach is appropriate for the type of person represented: a clergyman should be painted highlighting his eyes and lips and the mouth which he uses to speak, and a marchesa should be painted as a member of the world in which she holds her position. At some point in the discussion you might bring up someone they all have heard about and ask them to discuss how it would be appropriate to paint that person's portrait. In order to prepare the students for looking at the paintings, the handout asks what features the students look for, whether individual characteristics or context. Help the students with words they don't know (a marchesa is like a princess, a clergyman is a pastor or priest). They will notice that the clothing is dated, but it's not necessary to make an issue of it.

TWO PORTRAITS:

Portrait of a Clergyman, (Student vol., p. 39)
by **Albrecht Dürer**
Marchesa Brigida Spinola Doria,
by **Sir Peter Rubens**

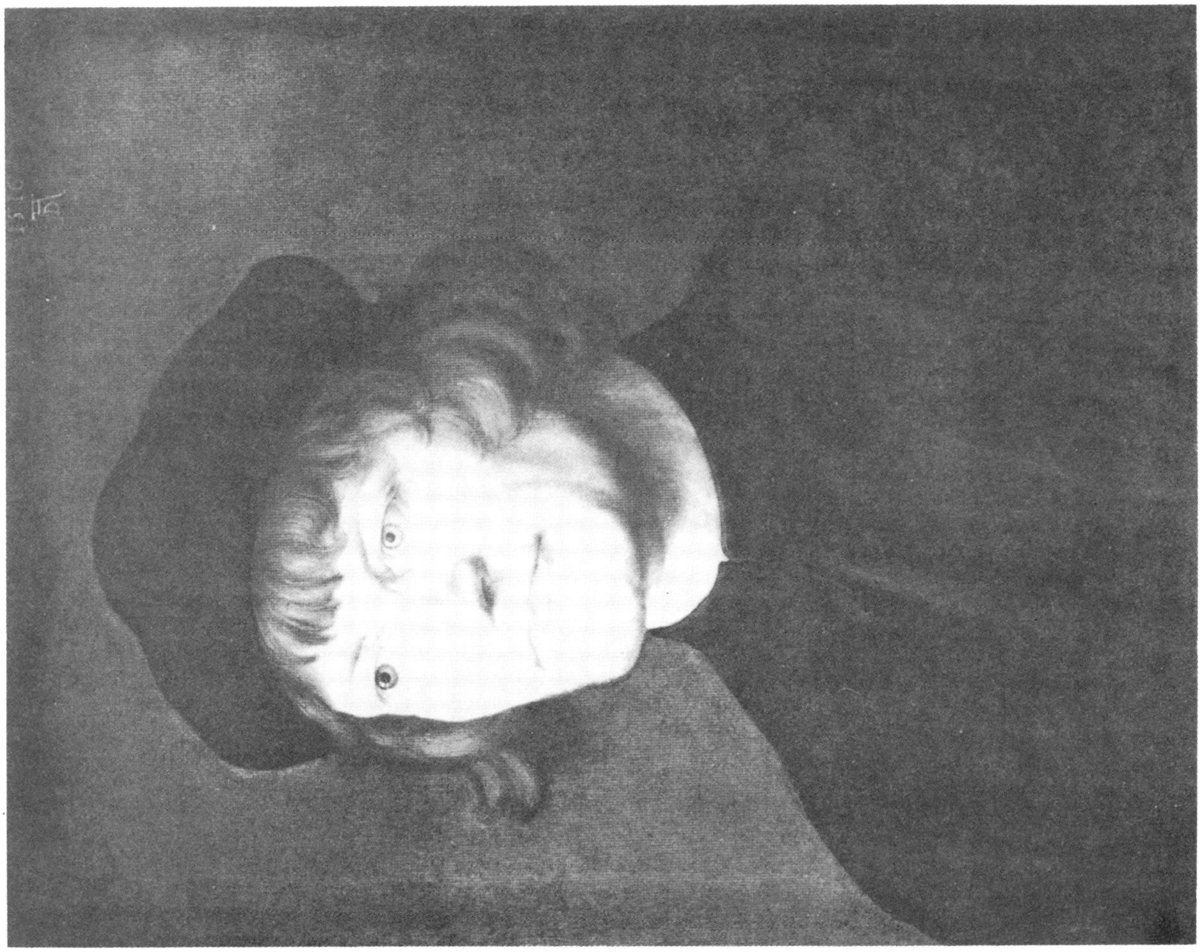

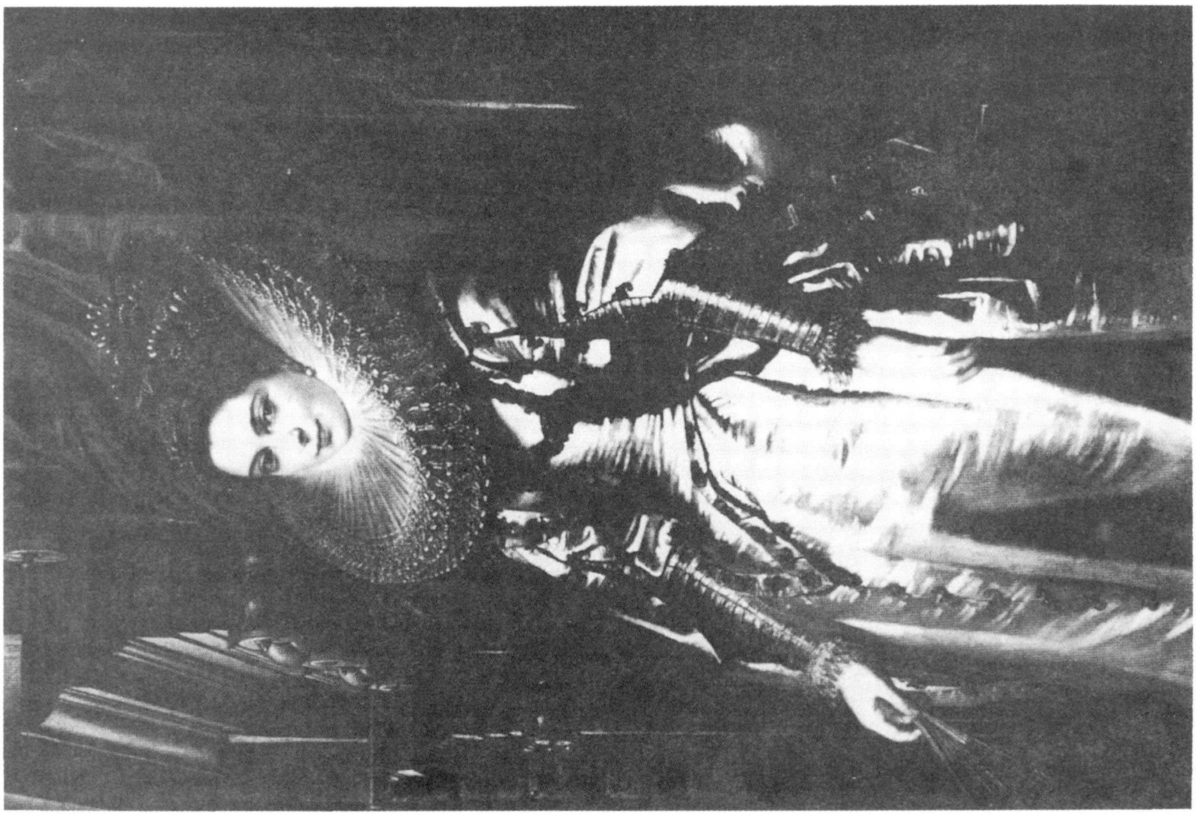

HANDOUT FOR CLASS #15

1. If you want to find out as much as you can about a person just by looking, what are the best clues? Listed below are four clues you might find useful. Put them in order of usefulness or importance (mark them 1 to 4: 1 is most useful, 4 is least). Add one of your own ideas.

    a. skin (smooth, wrinkled, etc?) _____
    b. eyes (big, drooping, bright, etc?) _____
    c. how they stand or sit _____
    d. the clothes they wear _____
    My own idea of what to look at:

2. a. If you are taking a photograph of someone you really want to remember, which of these would you do?
    a. Focus on the face?   yes( )   no( )
    b. Photograph the whole person?   yes( )   no( )
    c. Have them look directly at you?   yes( )   no( )
    d. Have them look a bit to the side?   yes( )   no( )
    e. Have them stand in a place
       that is special to you both.   yes( )   no( )

    b. For one of your "yes" answers, be able to give a reason.

ACTIVITIES FOR CLASS #15

1. Have the students sit in a circle. Pass out the handouts. Ask them to answer both questions.

2. Break the class into small groups of 4-5 and ask them to discuss their answers. They might begin this by taking turns saying what feature they look at and how they would photograph. Encourage them to give reasons for their yes answers.

3. Gather them all back into the large circle and show them the portraits. Ask them first to name what they see in each. Ask them whether they like one better and why. If it is appropriate and there is time, mention one or two well-known people and ask how their portrait should be painted or how they should be photographed. Should the portrait or photograph focus on the face or the whole person in a setting?

(These times are approximate only)

1. Sit in circle	1 min.
2. Handouts: answer both questions	6 mins.
3. Small-group discussion	10 mins.
4. Look at portraits	5 mins.
5. Discuss portrait differences	<u>18 mins.</u>
	40 mins.

Class #16   *The Republic,*
                                    by Plato

Summary/Purpose:

How we behave in public (for example, at school) can be very different from how we behave when alone, in the privacy of our own home. Someone who dresses up for school may prefer more casual clothes at home, while a child who is difficult at home may be well-behaved and agreeable in the classroom. As teachers, you may even have had the experience of meeting your students at the grocery store and realizing how surprised they are to see you there, as if you only existed as a public person. In this lesson, students will explore how they behave differently in private and in public. They probably think of themselves as always and everywhere the same, but all students will be able to supply experiences of changing themselves to match the circumstances. For example, they may not even feel tempted to turn on the TV if a parent has forbidden it and is nearby, but the desire to turn it on may become overwhelming if that parent has to leave the house unexpectedly on a short errand.

Socrates tells the story of a ring that makes its wearer invisible to illustrate his point that people behave well primarily because they fear being seen. He tells of a shepherd who discovers a magic ring that not only renders him invisible but also forgotten, so that no one can even be aware that he has suddenly become invisible. Socrates tells us that the shepherd used this power to commit many crimes and eventually overthrow the government. Given the ability to do what we want and not suffer any of the consequences of being seen, Socrates suggests that most people, perhaps all people, are not honest and well-behaved because they are good but because they are afraid of being seen by others. Your students may disagree with what Socrates says and indeed he is only bringing this up as a suggestion. They may think that some people behave well whether people see them or not. You should encourage them to bring up examples that would make Socrates reconsider his claim.

The Touchstones discussion class itself is a concrete example of this problem. In fact, it can present a dilemma for students. For the students in Touchstones speak in public, and that pressure alone can make students say what they think others expect them to say. However, the opposite is also a possibility. Some students who are very serious about what they think might say exactly what they are thinking as if they were talking to themselves. Behaving or speaking in public just as you would in private can also cause problems. Part of the work of Touchstones is to enable students to talk about things that really matter without making them so intensely personal or private that others are prevented from commenting.

Today's lesson begins that process by thinking about the issue of private and public behavior. The handout asks students to rank things they would or would not do with their parents present and watching. The idea of the exercise is that students see how their own behavior is often changed by the mere fact of being seen. In fact, the reason that all Touchstones discussions take place in a circle is so that no student can hide, so to speak. Being seen by everyone begins a long process that culminates in students taking responsibility for what they say and for what goes on in discussion. How to speak in such a public way is an issue your students have been dealing with throughout the year. It would be useful to hear whether they speak differently in Touchstones discussions compared with how they speak to their friends; that is, have these two types of speaking, one much more public than the other, started to come closer to one another?

The Republic, (Student vol., p. 41)
by Plato

Are people good because they want to be? Or are they good because they are afraid to be bad? To answer these questions let us pretend we can give both the good and the bad person the freedom and power to do whatever they please. Then in our imaginations we can see what they will do. I think the good person will be no different from the bad person, for he is really as selfish as the bad man. Only fear of the law makes him good. Let me tell you a story about a man who had such freedom.

People say that this man was a shepherd in the service of the king of Lydia. After a great rainstorm and an earthquake, the ground opened up where he was caring for sheep, and he went into the opening in the earth. The story goes on to say that he saw many wonderful things there, among which was a large bronze model of a horse with little doors on the side. When he looked in, he saw the body of a giant with a gold ring on its finger. He took the ring and left.

When the shepherds held their monthly meeting to report to the king about his flocks, he also attended, wearing the ring. While he was sitting there twisting the ring on his finger, he happened to turn it so that the stone faced his palm. When he did this, the story goes on, he became invisible. Those who sat around him could no longer see him. They spoke about him as if he were not there. He was amazed and twisted his ring once more. When he turned the stone out, he became visible again. He tested this many times, and found that the ring really possessed this power of making him invisible when he wanted. So with the help of this ring, he committed many crimes and took over the kingdom.

Now suppose we have two such rings. Let's give one to a good person and the other to an evil person. It is hard to believe that even a good man would stop himself from stealing and doing all kinds of other bad things, if he knew he would never get caught.

HANDOUT FOR CLASS #16

1. If you were in a room where your parents could see you, which of the things below would you do? You can check that you wouldn't do it at all, that you might do it, that you would probably do it, or that you'd certainly do it.

   If my parents could see me - Use a ✓.

	No, I wouldn't do it.	Maybe	Probably	Yes, I'd do it
I'd watch TV before my homework was done				
I'd eat candy, not a healthy snack				
I'd be very noisy				
I'd tease someone				
I wouldn't pick up after myself				

2. How would you mark the boxes above if your parents could *not* see you -- use ✗ this time.

ACTIVITIES FOR CLASS #16

1. Ask the students to sit in a circle and read them the story, asking them to read it silently with you. Ask them whether they would like to be invisible.

2. After five minutes or so, pass out the handout. Read it to them, taking care to help them understand how they are to answer both questions.

3. Break them into small groups of 4-5 and ask them to compare their answers. Was there one action that consistently received a "No" or a "Yes" whether the parents saw or not? For which actions did most students mark the opposite when they filled out question #2?

4. Move back into the large group and ask them how being invisible like the shepherd is like doing things in secret. Why does the act of being seen by other people change what we'd like to do?

(These times are approximate only)

1. Sit in a circle	1 min.
2. Read story and discuss	5 mins.
3. Pass out handout and answer #1 and #2	5 mins.
4. Small-group discussion	12 mins.
5. Large-group discussion	<u>17 mins.</u>
	40 mins.

Class #17   *How to Catch a Thief,*
                  A Tale from China

Summary/Purpose:

In the last class, the students considered how they behaved or spoke differently in public and private situations. In this class we will consider a related issue, how to find out whether someone is saying what we want to hear (flattering us), whether someone is telling us what they want us to hear (lying to us), or whether they are telling us the truth. It is often very frustrating to have to decide among these possibilities. It can be so frustrating that we are tempted to believe that somehow we must force the truth out of someone either by some kind of physical force or by interrogating them. It seems obvious that physical force and other brutal forms of coercion are not reliable, yet such practices persist. Most people in pain will say anything to get it to stop. Some people will admit to crimes whether they did them or not, betray anyone whether they know them or not, create the story they are asked to whether true or not, and in short, speak or act in any way required to get the pain to stop. At any rate, even if some people were to resist, such methods are totally discredited simply *because* large numbers of people would "break" under such pressures and so give unreliable information. Asking questions is a better route but can also be unreliable. Sometimes we can trap someone into giving contradictory answers and so at least persuade ourselves that that person has not told the truth. But finding out what the truth is can be extremely problematic because of what we expect the person to say. Because we often hear only what we want to hear, we are clearly blocked from learning what the truth is. Therefore, we are back to the issue of how to tell if someone is telling the truth, especially when the stakes are high.

    The text for today's lesson tells the story of a wise judge who claims to be able to distinguish the truth from a lie without injuring or even questioning anyone. He does this by a trick. He says he has a bell which will ring when a thief touches it. Ultimately, one could say that his method involves an element of fear, the fear that the theft committed will cause the bell to ring and hence tell everyone of the person's guilt. Nevertheless, no physical harm takes place or is threatened. One of the questions which should be raised during the whole-class discussion is whether the students would approve of using the bell at all. That is, assuming the bell did in fact work, that it always rang when touched by a thief, would they ever use it? Should it be used to detect criminals? If they were a parent, would they use it on their children? Would they be willing to allow it to be used against themselves? In each case they should give their reasons. If the students don't see the connection themselves as the class period progresses, it should be explained that the bell is like a modern lie detector. How is it unlike one? If technology were able to improve the reliability of lie detectors, would the students approve of their use?

However, before raising these important questions in the large-group discussion, the students should engage in a practical exercise. This exercise should take place *before* the text is read to them and should take the following form. The handout tells them to choose two things about themselves: one is made-up but easily believable, the other is true but not easy to believe. In pairs, each should tell one of the two things. The other person should try to figure out if that thing is true or made-up. At the end of five minutes, the "truth" can really be told. In the large group, students should discuss the difficulties they had in trying to determine the truth of what they heard.

After about six or eight minutes of discussion, they should turn to the text for today and, after it is read to them, discuss whether the judge's method was a good one or whether the accused man was, in fact, truthful and honest. Finally, turn the discussion to those issues mentioned earlier in this summary.

How to Catch a Thief, (Student vol., p. 43)
A Tale from China

Many years ago a wise judge lived in a small village. People came to him from the whole country to get his help. It was said he could solve a crime without ever questioning a suspect or without hurting or torturing a person until he confessed. He believed both ways of getting information were not really useful. If you hurt someone, that person will often say whatever is needed to get you to stop. If you question someone, you often hear what you want the suspect to say. So he always looked for ways to trap a suspect so that he could be sure to solve the crime.

One day a great king came to him with all his assistants. He knew that one of them had stolen a valuable jewel, but the king and all his wise men could not figure out which one.

When the king told the judge his problem, the great judge said, "Nearby is a temple which contains a bell that has wonderful powers. When a man who has not stolen touches it, the bell remains silent. However, it rings when it is touched by a thief." The king was delighted. He explained the test to his assistants and sent them all to the temple.

The judge had the bell placed behind a curtain in a small room and covered its surface with ink. He then took each of the suspects to the room and had them put their hands through the curtain to touch the bell. When they took their hands out, the judge and the king examined them. Everyone's hands were stained except for one man. This man was arrested and questioned. However, he kept saying he was not a thief. Even when he was beaten and tortured he did not confess. But the king was convinced he was guilty and had him sent to jail for many years.

HANDOUT FOR CLASS #17

Write two things about yourself under (a) and (b) below. One should be true, but the other false. ***Do not mark them true or false, nor put them in any special order.*** Make the false one something that someone *could* believe and the true one something about you that people in class might find hard to believe.

a)

b)

ACTIVITIES FOR CLASS #17

1. Ask the students to sit in a circle. Pass out the handout. Help them to understand what is asked. The students are to write down two things about themselves, one true, and the other false. Naturally, for it to be difficult, the false thing should be easily believable and the true thing somehow unlikely. For instance, a student could say (falsely) that a famous singer is a relative or that (truly) they once met a famous baseball player. Give them time to decide what to write. If you wish, go around and help each student. Ask them to put their name on the paper.

2. Pair up all the students (preferably not putting best friends together; use one group of three if necessary). Have each student select either (a) or (b) from the handout to tell their partner. Give the pairs about 10 minutes to try to find out whether each other's statement is true or false. Tell each student that when they are questioned they have to try to fool the questioner. After that time, have each person guess and let each writer reveal whether it was true or false.

3. Move them back into a large circle and discuss with them what made the exercise difficult or easy.

4. Read the story and ask whether they think the bell is a useful method and how they would have approached the problem.

(These times are approximate only)

1. Sit in circle	1 min.
2. Pass out handout; students write true and false things	8 mins.
3. Student pairs (5 mins. each)	10 mins.
4. Large-group discussion of exercise	5 mins.
5. Read story and discuss	<u>16 mins.</u>
	40 mins.

Class #18   *Definitions of a Straight Line*

Summary/Purpose:

In the many cases of perspective that we have considered, the following issue frequently came up: what underlying object is implied by the different points of view? However, in this week's class we confront a different kind of case. In this lesson, we all agree on the object but differ on how best to characterize it. This means that we disagree on what best describes that object or on the relative importance of its characteristics. A somewhat similar case came up earlier in the year. This was the Winslow Homer painting *Hound and Hunter*. In that lesson the students all saw the same reproduction but came up with a variety of different stories. These different stories were probably mutually exclusive in the sense that, although students may have felt one was clearly best, other points of view might still be considered plausible. Yet, there is another case where everyone agrees that the differing accounts are all correct and thus that the choice among them must be based on grounds other than correctness. This lesson will therefore bring to the surface that, depending on our purpose, one particular viewpoint may be more or less appropriate than others.

We will explore this type of situation by considering a simple geometrical object that will be familiar to all your students. This object is a straight line. From our very first drawings as children, we become familiar with straight lines and with how hard it is to draw them. All of our students are expert at recognizing them and are very proficient at deciding that a particular line is not straight either because it is curved or bent. They are probably also very skilled at deciding that one line is straighter than another. Yet, in spite of this high informal level of expertise, it is very difficult to describe a straight line. In fact, it is one of the most difficult objects to define. Different people can well have different ideas about what is crucial in the straightness of a straight line. All of these ideas may in fact be equally correct geometrically and yet quite different from one another. Some people might choose the way the line looks, its quality; others might select its quantity or length, the fact that it is the shortest distance between two points. Still others might select the fact that it is unique, that you can only draw one straight line between two points, whereas every other line between two points has a symmetrical match. For example, every curved line between two points has a mirror image line as in diagram #4. Each of these descriptions is correct about the very same object, a straight line. Yet how should we choose among them? Which is the correct point of view or is each one appropriate for a particular purpose? One description might be best for actually drawing a straight line, one might be best for deciding whether a line is actually straight, one best for teaching someone what a straight line is, and another best for deciding which of two non-straight lines is straighter. What the class can explore is how a particular purpose can determine the point of view one adopts.

In the handout, the students will remind themselves of two skills they already have. In question #1 they are asked to draw a straight line. They should first do this without using any straightedge like a ruler or the side of a book. Then they will redraw a straight line using some aid like the side of a book or pencil, a tight piece of string, or even a ruler. The question you should explore with them is why it was hard to draw a straight line freehand. Then have them answer question #3. This exercise will give them some experience in deciding when one line is straighter than others. In the large-group discussion on the definitions you will, as in class #13, act more like your role in a regular class. You should be more active about assisting them to understand each of the definitions and have them be clear that each definition does in fact describe a straight line. As you are helping them with this, encourage them to bring up reasons why some definitions are better or worse, harder or easier to understand. Definition #1 gives an important characteristic of a straight line, that it is the shortest distance between two points. However, some people might claim that this definition helps you draw a straight line but doesn't explain what it is to be straight. Definition #2 shows how straight lines differ from other lines which would move when rotated. This wouldn't help us draw a straight line but might be a useful test to determine if a line is straight. Definition #3, looking down the straight line and only seeing a point does not really give you a test or a method to draw it but might be the most useful in explaining what a straight line is like. Definition #4, which says that only one straight line can be drawn between two points, might be most useful in doing geometry. These are just possible uses for each definition, and your students may have others. What is important is for them to see that the same object can be described in different and useful ways. This week's class once again employs discussion to talk about content.

Definitions of a Straight Line   (Student vol., p. 45)

Ever since you were very young, you have probably been drawing pictures. Some of these were of animals or trees, other drawings were of buildings. Surprisingly, when we look at these pictures, we realize that the hardest thing to draw is a perfectly straight line. Since a straight line is the simplest line there is, this might puzzle us. In addition, though it is easy to tell if a line is not straight, it is very hard to tell if a line is perfectly straight even when we draw it with a ruler.

In this class, we will consider four different ways of explaining to someone how we would decide if a line is perfectly straight. We will discuss which way is best or whether you can think up better ones.

1. A straight line is the shortest distance between two points.

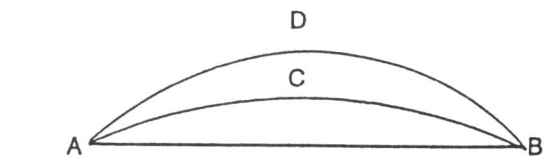

    Line AB is shorter than line ACB and line ACB is shorter than ADB. If line AB is shortest of all lines between A and B, it is perfectly straight.

2. Imagine a straight line and a curved line drawn between points A and B on a piece of paper. If you spin the paper around points A and B, the curved line moves but the straight line doesn't.

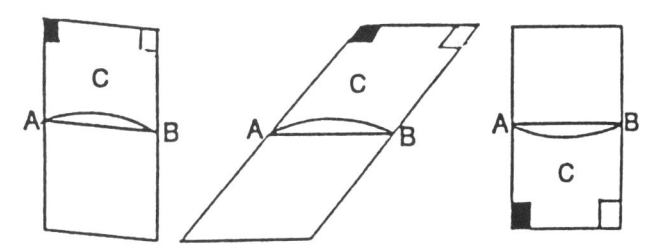

    As the paper turns (follow marks ■ and □), straight line AB doesn't move but curved line ACB does move.

3. If you look down a straight line, you only see a point and no other part of that straight line.

Look along Straight line AB

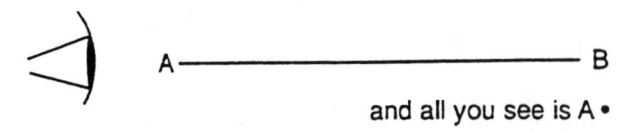

A————————————B

and all you see is A •

4. Between any two points, such as points A and B, you can draw only one straight line.

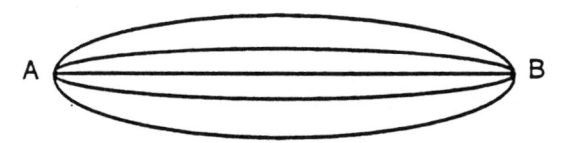

There is only one possible straight line, AB

HANDOUT FOR CLASS #18

1. Draw a straight line without any help.

2. Draw a straight line using any help or aid (like a ruler or book) you have with you.

3. Which of the following lines is straighter between points A and B? Circle the one you choose.

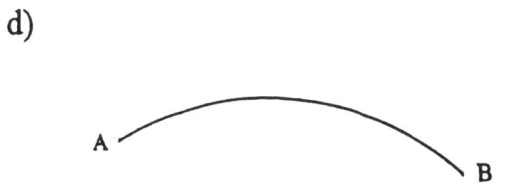

a)

b)

c)

d)

93

ACTIVITIES FOR CLASS #18

1. Ask your students to sit in a circle. Pass out the handout. Have them first draw a straight line freehand. Then allow them to draw a second line using any convenient straightedge. Ask them why it is difficult to draw a straight line.

2. Ask your students to separate into small groups of 4-5 and agree on an answer to question #3. Tell them they should have a reason for their choice.

3. Reconvene the large group and have the small group report. As they report, remind them to tell how they decided which was the straightest.

4. Show them the four descriptions and make sure that they understand them by considering the illustrations. You may wish to explain any they have trouble with. Make sure that they know that each description is legitimate. Ask them which description is most useful for drawing a straight line. Is any best for deciding whether a line is straight? Can they think of any other descriptions of straight lines?

(These times are approximate only)

1. Sit in circle; draw lines on handout	5 mins.
2. Small groups; answer question #3	10 mins.
3. Large group; small-group reports	10 mins.
4. Definitions and discussion	<u>15 mins.</u>
	40 mins.

Class #19

Gilgamesh the King,
An Epic from Ancient Persia

Summary/Purpose:

What makes it possible for us to learn from other people? Must they be just like us in some important way? This is the assumption of many self-help groups, where support and counsel are provided by people who have experienced just what the person in trouble is going through. Or can we and our students learn from a wide range of people: friends, teachers, parents, strangers, and even enemies? Though it is clear that we teachers, and even strangers, can teach students many things, can we help them face the deepest difficulties they may have in learning?

There is no doubt that everyone has to learn important things about themselves. Sometimes we can learn these lessons on our own, by the act of identifying with others and imagining how our behavior affects them. More often, however, we need the help of other people to get a clear perspective on ourselves. Then we can see ourselves as others see us and either wish to change our behavior or our opinions or be confirmed in what we are doing. This experience lies at the heart of the Touchstones Discussion Project: we need other people to be able to learn about the world and even about ourselves. The key question is who can assist us, whose point of view are we willing to accept to learn something we have not noticed about ourselves?

The ancient epic story of Gilgamesh explores this issue. Gilgamesh is a very powerful king who has no compassion for his own people. He works them so hard that they haven't time enough to tend to the welfare of their own families. He treats them just as he pleases and apparently does not see it as wrong or cruel. The story implies that Gilgamesh will only listen to someone he considers his equal. In the first part of the story, Gilgamesh lacks such a person, a kind of "second self," someone he respects enough to listen to the most candid talk about his own faults. He finds such a person in the forest man. The forest man is very different in upbringing and attitudes; for instance, he frees the animals caught in Gilgamesh's snares. But physically he could be the king's twin. Gilgamesh's first impulse on seeing the forest man is to fight him. When he finds that he cannot defeat him, Gilgamesh stops the fight and offers his friendship: here at last is a man he can respect. However, the forest man replies that before they can be friends, Gilgamesh must become a just and caring king to his people. Gilgamesh laughs and agrees, and does in fact become a great king. The forest man then becomes his great ally and friend.

Few of us like to admit that we need the kind of help that Gilgamesh so clearly needs. The Touchstones Discussion Project acknowledges that even the very talented need the help of others. For everyone brings strengths and weaknesses to discussion; everyone depends on the other members of the group to temper their strengths and overcome their weaknesses. For example, careful readers may need to learn to explore ideas with others; acute listeners may need to develop the ability to speak out; articulate speakers may need to learn how to listen. Discussion is not meant to be a test of strength, but students may well debate each other initially in exactly that way before they settle down to discussion with people they now can see as equals.

In the story, although the people of Ur see the forest man and Gilgamesh as equals, the king only accepts their equality after a test of strength. However, the forest man requires more than equality of strength. He will only respect Gilgamesh if the king changes his behavior and becomes caring and just. Some of your students will be like Gilgamesh, some like the forest man. The handout will assist them in determining who they are like and what they require to respect and learn from another person. A goal of Touchstones is to create enough mutual respect that students who normally do not associate with each other can in fact tell each other important things and help one another learn. To achieve that, students need to explore how and when they are likely to listen to others, and whether it is possible to hear these truths about themselves from those who are not their "second selves."

Gilgamesh the King, (Student vol., p. 47)
An Epic from Ancient Persia

Gilgamesh was a very cruel ruler of the city called Uruk. He made his people work such long hours that they had very little time to gather food for themselves or take care of their families. The people of Uruk were very unhappy and prayed for help for many years. Finally, their prayers were answered. A man appeared who was as strong as Gilgamesh and who in fact looked just like the evil king. He lived in the forest and soon became a good friend to all the animals. One day, one of the king's hunters saw this man undoing the animal traps that the king had set and he ran back to tell Gilgamesh. The king became very angry and had soldiers bring this forest man into the city.

When the people saw the man of the forest, they thought he was Gilgamesh because he was so proud and handsome and strong. However, they were startled when their king came out of the palace. They looked at these two men, who could have been twins, and held their breath, not knowing what would happen.

Gilgamesh raced forward and hit the forest man in the face. However, the forest man jumped right back up from the ground and struck the king in the chest. The king had never been hit that hard before and fell down. The two men kept fighting, but neither could defeat the other. Finally the king said, "Enough! Why are we fighting? We are equal in strength and we look like brothers. You are my second self. Come, let us be friends and stand together against the enemies of my people."

The forest man got up from the ground and offered his hand to help Gilgamesh. "If we are to be true friends, you must hear my words. I will stand with you against the enemies of your people, but right now you yourself are their greatest enemy. We can be friends only if you become a just and caring king. Otherwise we must keep on fighting, and, as you can see, neither of us can beat the other."

Gilgamesh was so amazed that he stood there with his mouth wide open. He looked as though he had been struck by lightning. He was such a mighty king that no one had ever spoken to him like that before. Even if someone had tried to give him advice, the king wouldn't have listened because no one was his equal. A smile crossed Gilgamesh's face and he began to laugh. He stretched out his hand to his equal and followed the words of his new friend.

HANDOUT FOR CLASS #19

1. Suppose you were mean to one of your friends. Maybe you spread a story about them. Who could persuade you to apologize and yet make you feel good about it? Choose from the list below:

    ☐ My parents
    ☐ My sister or brother
    ☐ My best friend
    ☐ The person I was mean to
    ☐ Someone I didn't know very well who saw it happen
    ☐ A friend of the person I was mean to
    ☐ Other

2. What kind of person can best persuade you that you have done something wrong and should apologize? Check all the boxes that apply.

    ☐ Someone who is my age
    ☐ Someone who is a boy like me or a girl like me
    ☐ Someone who is a good student
    ☐ Someone who is fair
    ☐ Someone who lives near me
    ☐ Someone who usually tells me good things about myself
    ☐ Someone who likes to play the same games
    ☐ Someone who is a relative (brother, sister, cousin, etc.)
    ☐ Someone who is the same size as me
    ☐ Someone from the same kind of family

ACTIVITIES FOR CLASS #19

1. Ask the students to sit in a circle. Pass out the handout. Ask them to answer both questions. You should read the questions to them and answer any questions they might have. The object is for them to identify someone who could criticize them but in such a way that they could accept it.

2. Break the class into small groups of 4-5 and ask them to share their answers to question #1 with each other. After a few minutes, ask them to try to agree on two responses to question #2.

3. Ask your students to come back into the large circle and have the small groups report on the two items they agreed on. Make a list of all the items to see if one item is on everyone's list. Let the class as a whole discuss this as the reports are given, but make sure every group reports.

4. Read the story and let the students read along silently. Begin the discussion by asking why they think Gilgamesh listened to the forest man. This will encourage them to begin with evidence from the story itself. As the discussion continues, ask them if they could imagine some other character, different from the forest man, who could persuade the king not to be so cruel. Toward the end, ask them what kinds of things they can best learn from strangers, friends, or classmates.

(These times are approximate only)

1. Sit in circle and pass out handout	2 mins.
2. Answer handout questions	5 mins.
3. Small-group work	7 mins.
4. Large circle; list qualities	10 mins.
5. Read story	3 mins.
6. Discuss story	13 mins.
	40 mins.

Class #20   *The Weapons of King Chuko,*
              by Lo Kuan Chung

Summary/Purpose:

In order to participate successfully in discussions, people must explore what is appropriate to say, and also how and when to say it. During this year, the students have investigated a number of aspects of language which are relevant to discussions. They have experimented with the relation of form and content, and examined the differences between objective opinions and facts. In addition, they have practiced how to give and accept criticism, how to ask questions, and how to explain their ideas. In other words, they have considered what to say and how it should be presented. In this week's meeting, they will focus on the third aspect of language, when, if ever, something should be said. They will do this by viewing a familiar situation which involves the issue of bragging.

It is very difficult for any of us to keep our successes in life secret. In fact, many people are tempted to boast of success, to flaunt it. It is true that in some societies it is not socially acceptable to boast. In the Unites States we are ambivalent about boasting and its counterpart, modesty. Winning, outsmarting others, and being on top are such a premium in America that those who reach pinnacles of success in business, sports, or entertainment are held in high esteem and are expected to flaunt their status to quite a considerable degree. On the other hand, "showing off" and "blowing our own horn" are still phrases of rebuke. Someone who wears success and wealth with grace instead of ostentation is still admired by many people.

These conflicting values are very present to elementary school students. They neither want their successes overlooked nor do they want to be called a "show-off." They must decide when, if ever, they broadcast their accomplishments. Indeed, students confront this conflict in their school life. For example, a student may do especially well on a test and be rightly proud. But if they reveal that success through their own excitement or shouts of joy in class, they might turn their fellow students against them, either for excelling at the "wrong" thing or by implying that they are better than the others. That can be a difficult and delicate situation for successful students. In the same way, the students who are successful in sports may get acclaim from others up to a point, but it can backfire if they are overly boastful. Then they risk being viewed as "dumb jocks."

The handout for this class highlights the problems arising from this tension by giving the students choices between degrees whether they would tell or keep secret certain facts about themselves which most people would consider admirable. The small-group work will give them the opportunity to explore *why* they wish to tell certain things but not other things. In particular, they should be invited to try to understand how and when justifiable pride can be freely expressed or restrained, so that it is better told by someone else.

The text for today exhibits the special case of King Chuko, who knows he is clever, thoughtful, and shrewd, but who is not boastful or explicitly proud. On the contrary, he acts modestly and deliberatively even to the point of appearing careless. His city is threatened by a large army and by cleverness he thwarts the attack. However, after the enemy is successfully fooled by the king's trick, he refuses to be praised and stops his subjects from celebrating. In one sense, the king must order the quiet modesty to continue for the sake of the safety of the city, but do the students think they could have held back from celebrating forever? Do they admire this king's restraint? What would happen in the future if all the people celebrated? What would happen if a few months later the enemy general learned there had been a trick played on him?

The Weapons of King Chuko, (Student vol., p. 49)
by Lo Kuan Chung

Chuko was a great king, famous in war and loved by his people. His enemy, the king of a neighboring country, sent two great armies to destroy him. When the news came that two armies were approaching the city, all of his people were upset and afraid because their king had very few soldiers there. But King Chuko was calm. He sent a soldier to get some things for him and went to wait on the highest wall of the city. Soon the soldier brought him what he asked for: a colorful robe and a musical instrument. "Now I have the weapons I need," he said. Everyone was puzzled and afraid. "Now, do everything I say," King Chuko told his few soldiers. "Take down all the flags, open the city gates very wide, let some people go outside to work, and keep out of sight." Everyone thought he had lost his mind from fear, but they followed his orders.

Soon the enemy armies halted some distance from the city, and the general and his officers spied on the city from a nearby hill. They saw King Chuko on the high wall, beautifully dressed, playing the instrument and singing, the city gate open, and people working peacefully. His officers were eager to attack. One said "Look, we will win a great victory. They don't expect us. We will destroy them." The general was silent and studied King Chuko and the city. Finally, after much thought, he said, "Tell my armies to march north and to stay 20 miles away from the city." "What?" said a young prince. "We must attack now."

"You are here to learn about war and this is your first lesson," said the general. "King Chuko must think I'm a great fool. He thinks I will fall into his trap. A great army is hidden in the city waiting to attack us." "How can you tell?" asked the prince. The general replied, "See the workers outside the city? King Chuko would never risk his citizens' lives."

After the armies left, King Chuko stopped singing and playing and came down from the city wall. All his people were amazed at the success of his weapons. They all wanted to celebrate. But their king refused to let them. "No, we must not celebrate. We must look sad. What if our enemy sends scouts to watch the city? If we celebrate, they'll learn it wasn't a trap but a trick. Next time they will destroy us. This is a victory we must always keep a secret."

HANDOUT FOR CLASS #20

1. Which of the following would you be so proud of that you would want to tell your friends and everyone else about it? Check the box under "Yes, I'd tell." From this same group there may be other things you would *not* want to tell everyone. Check the box under "No, I'd keep it a secret."

	Yes, I'd tell	No, I'd keep it a secret
a. You win a big trophy in sports.	☐	☐
b. You live in a fine, large house with servants.	☐	☐
c. You score highest grades on a state test.	☐	☐
d. Your parent is very famous.	☐	☐
e. You just received $500 from your relative.	☐	☐
f. You are the strongest person in school.	☐	☐
g. You play a musical instrument so well you win a prize.	☐	☐
h. You are named "most beautiful" or "most handsome" in a contest.	☐	☐
i. You save someone's life.	☐	☐

2. Is there one item on this list that you would want people to find out about you, but only from someone else? Put the letter of it here _____.

ACTIVITIES FOR CLASS #20

1. Ask the students to sit in a circle. Pass out the handout. Have the students answer the questions. Make sure they understand the questions and what they are to do. If they can't mark yes or no easily, tell them to pick the best one and go on.

2. Form them into small groups of 4 or 5 and ask them to share their answers. Ask them why some things are appropriate to tell everyone about and some aren't. Why is bragging bad? When is it bad? Always? In particular ask them to explain why they preferred some things to be told by someone else.

3. Ask them to return to the circle and read the story to them. Have them read it silently. Ask them if King Chuko was right to keep his victory a secret and whether they think that the people would be able to. Would it be OK to celebrate if King Chuko had won a great battle and made the enemy armies run home? Finally ask them what item on the list is most like what happened to King Chuko.

(These times are approximate only)

1. Sit in circle	1 min.
2. Pass out handout; answer #1 and #2	7 mins.
3. Small-group work	14 mins.
4. Read story & discuss	<u>18 mins.</u>
	40 mins.

Class #21   *The Odyssey,*
                              by Homer

Summary/Purpose:

One of the hardest things to understand is why a person does something in a specific way. When we see or hear about what a person has done, we often ask ourselves what we would have done in that situation. We are tempted to judge that an action makes sense if we could imagine doing the same thing in the same case. However, we hardly ever judge our own actions this way. We are so familiar with the situation and what we did that we don't analyze it unless someone calls it to our attention. Our familiarity makes it almost impossible to ask ourselves why *we* do certain things. However, when someone else's action puzzles us, we probe more deeply into why they did that specific thing or behaved that way. These puzzling situations also force us to ask ourselves, sometimes for the first time, how we would have acted differently. By exploring this contrast, we can make explicit the reasons for our own actions.

When we first hear about an action which puzzles us, we may dismiss it: that is, we may claim that person is just silly or foolish. This allows us to avoid trying to figure out why someone did something puzzling. Calling someone silly or foolish is an easy and cheap way of saying that person had no justification for their action, that there were no good reasons for what they did. However, if we are forced to consider it more closely, we can often enter into the perspective of the other person. As we do, that person frequently seems less foolish or silly than we thought.

Entering into this person's perspective, of course, involves overcoming a greater or lesser difference between that person and ourselves. It may be simply that we thought an action was strange because we didn't have enough information. Suppose someone gave $10,000 to another person. If we thought this person was unknown to the benefactor, such an action would puzzle us. However, if we discovered that the recipient had long ago helped the donor's family, it would begin to make sense. But what if we could not discover any previous connection between the two people? In order to make sense of this action, we would have to enter more deeply into the perspective, the goals and motives of the donor in order to avoid considering that person merely silly or foolish. Doing this would also make our own goals and purposes explicit. Today's reading will present the students with the possibility of exploring this.

    Much of the story about the Greek hero Odysseus and the Cyclops seems to show Odysseus as foolish or silly. However, some incidents in the tale also indicate how clever he is. How can he be so clever and yet so foolish? This dilemma makes it possible to think that maybe he was *not* being foolish. The acts that seem foolish are going into a strange cave to see if he can get a gift, calling out to the blinded cyclops when he and his men have escaped, and then calling out a second time even after they were almost hit by a boulder and killed. The clever actions are Odysseus telling the Cyclops that his name was No One and figuring out a way to escape from the cave. The question students should discuss is how the same person who did the clever things could have done the seemingly foolish things. You should also encourage them to bring up cases where they once thought someone did something foolish and later reconsidered their opinion. What did they find out that made them change their minds?

The Odyssey, (Student vol., p. 51)
by Homer

    Odysseus and his men were tired and nearly starving from their long journey across the sea. When they reached an island, they hunted, ate, and rested. The next day, after a long sleep, Odysseus saw another rocky island nearby. "I think that is where the Cyclopes live. I have always wanted to see these giant creatures." At first they tried to stop him, but after a while twelve of Odysseus' men agreed. They rowed to the island and climbed a high cliff to reach a cave.

    The cave was bigger than ten houses. In the back of the cave, they found some sheep, and a great deal of cheese and other food. They all ate their fill and wanted to leave. But Odysseus refused. "No, I want to meet the Cyclops, the owner of this cave. He may give a present to a stranger visiting him." Soon the ground shook, and a giant with only one eye in the center of his forehead stood at the entrance. He was bigger than they could ever have imagined. He easily rolled a huge stone across the mouth of the cave. Odysseus thought it would take 100 men to move that stone.

    The giant saw the men standing as far away as they could in great fear. "Who are you? Are you pirates?" asked the Cyclops. "No, we are soldiers traveling home from war," answered Odysseus. "We ask for kindness, the kindness all men give to strangers and travelers." "What do I care what others do," said the Cyclops, as he grabbed two men, killed them, and ate them. Then the giant fell asleep. Odysseus stood his ground, filled with anger. "I could kill him now," he thought, "but then we could never move that rock. We would be trapped." The next morning the Cyclops awoke, killed two more men, ate them, and then started his day. He moved the great rock, counted all his sheep as they ran to the fields, and then put the rock back as he left. As he watched, Odysseus thought of a plan.

He found a large stick belonging to the giant. It was more than six feet long. He sharpened one end and hid the stick. When the Cyclops returned, he killed two more men. Hiding his anger and disgust, Odysseus said, "You must be very thirsty now." Odysseus offered the giant a very strong wine he had brought with him. The giant loved it and kept drinking. "Stranger, tell me your name so I can thank you." "My name is No One," said Odysseus. The Cyclops replied, "Well, No One, my present to you is that I will kill you last." He laughed, drank some more wine, and fell asleep.

Moving quickly, Odysseus and his men took the sharp stick and pushed it into the giant's one eye, blinding him. He screamed in horrible pain. Other Cyclopes came running to his cave and yelled in, "What's wrong? Is someone hurting you?"

"No One is in here! No One is trying to kill me!" When they heard this they said, "If no one is hurting you, you must be sick. Get some rest," they said, leaving him alone. The giant screamed in pain all night. In the morning, the Cyclops moved the rock and let the sheep out. Once they were out, he said, "Now I'll find you and kill you all." But he heard Odysseus calling him from outside, for he had already escaped and was in his boat. He and his men had hung on to the wool of the sheep's bellies and gotten away.

They could have gotten away safely, but Odysseus yelled to the Cyclops, "You should have been kinder to your guests!" At the sound of his voice, the giant threw a large rock at the boat and almost crushed it. The men rowed hard and got even farther away. Odysseus stood up to call out again. His men tried to stop him, but he wouldn't listen. "Cyclops, if anyone asks who blinded you, say it was Odysseus, King of Ithaca."

The Cyclops went crazy with anger and prayed to his father, the ruler of the sea. "Father, hurt Odysseus for what he has done to me. Make him suffer on his trip home." The giant's father heard him. To punish Odysseus, all his men were killed in storms and accidents, and he got home only after ten years of hardship and pain.

HANDOUT FOR CLASS #21

1. A man runs into a burning house. Below are some of the reasons he might give. Which ones seem silly to you? Check the box if they seem silly reasons to you.

    1. ☐ He is trying to save his mother.
    2. ☐ He is trying to save his pet dog.
    3. ☐ He is trying to save his tropical fish.
    4. ☐ He is trying to save a chair.
    5. ☐ He is trying to save a picture.
    6. ☐ he is trying to show how brave he is.
    7. ☐ He is trying to put out the fire.

2. In your small group, take *one* of the ones you marked silly and make up a reason so that it's not silly anymore.

ACTIVITIES FOR CLASS #21

1. Ask your students to sit in a circle. Pass out the handout. Ask them to answer question #1 individually.

2. Divide them into small groups of 4-5 and have them (1) agree on one of the seven that they all believe is silly and (2) have them work together on #2 to make up a plausible reason so that what the man did is not silly anymore. For example, if students thought it was silly to save a chair (#4), a reason that would change that perception might be that the chair is a very valuable antique or that it was made for the man by his father.

3. Ask them to return them to the large group. Have the small group report on the reasons they came up with. Then read them the story. The story should be clear, but feel free to clarify any facts. Begin by having the students help you make two lists, one of all the smart things that Odysseus does and another of all the silly things he does. Write them on the blackboard. Let the whole class thoroughly discuss each point—some may see an act as silly when others see it as brave or smart.

4. Begin the discussion by asking the class how someone who is so clever can also be so silly. Can they think of any reasons that might make sense of the silly things?

(These times are approximate only)

1. Form circle; handout question #1	5 mins.
2. Small-group work on question #2	7 mins.
3. Small-group reports	6 mins.
4. Read story and make lists	7 mins.
5. Discussion	15 mins.
	40 mins.

Class #22   *How Much is a Son Worth?,*
                     A Tale from Saudi Arabia

Summary/Purpose:

We all fill private and public roles. We are wives, husbands, sisters, or brothers at home, but teachers, principals, or counselors at work. Adults experience this duality every day, but it will still be new to your students. They will at least know that their public roles as students require them to undertake responsibilities and duties unlike those at home. For example, as students, they live by regimented schedules, they study subjects they may not even like at the moment, and they must control their impulses, doing what others tell them to do rather than what they prefer. By contrast, in their private lives as children in families, they enjoy much more freedom to do as they wish. It is very important for them to reflect on this duality. This week's text presents this opposition in a vivid way.

The story tells of a prince who takes his son on a trip to learn about the world. While they are in a market area, the father lets his son go off to explore on his own. However, he is kidnapped and held for ransom. The prince wants his son back but his response is puzzling. He offers less ransom every day. The students, like the kidnapper, probably would expect the opposite. They would expect that as each day went by the prince would be more anxious about his son and thus prepared to offer much more money for his safe return. However, he doesn't. How can the prince so easily distinguish between the boy as his son and as someone who will rule? As he explains to the kidnapper, each day the boy is held captive diminishes his ability to become a great ruler. But how can the prince offer less money for his son's return than for the return of the boy he is training to rule after him? Why is the boy's worth (as the title asks) based on his public role and not his private role as a son? After all, he will succeed his father as prince precisely because he is his son. The story seems to say that the prince cannot be like other fathers, nor can the son of a prince be like other boys. Even as a child, he must behave as the prince he is destined to be.

It may be very hard for students to view the father sympathetically. You may have to help them by pointing out that their own parents can love them as their children but still be very upset with them if they don't abide by their public duty to study hard and do well in school. Some students may even have been told that not doing well in school may affect their future, a warning, of course, that they probably do not understand.

You should also encourage them to consider whether the prince was wrong about his analysis of the situation. Perhaps some of your students will think the boy will be even better as a prince after the captivity. Or were the decreasing amounts of money simply the clever trick of a prince to regain his son?

The tension between being a public and private person has come up frequently this year in the way people behave in discussion classes. The Touchstones Discussion Project requires that students accept a more overtly public role as a member of the discussion group. They must take responsibility for their own learning, for the overall success of the discussion, and for including everyone in their speaking and listening, even students they may not like. They cannot behave as they would like nor are there the usual devices, like hand raising, to help them remember what role they are occupying. Because the discussion lacks some of the formal features of a regular class, students will have to be more conscious and more deliberate about how they act toward others. The handout turns the students' attention to the discussion class itself and the skills that they are learning. In addition it will help them focus on some of the ways they need to improve during the rest of the year.

How Much is a Son Worth?, (Student vol., p. 55)
A Tale from Saudi Arabia

A prince took his son on a trip to study the habits of many people so that he would be the best ruler possible. In each country they looked first at the libraries and other great buildings, and then the market area. In one country, there were many shops in the market and it was crowded with thousands of people. It was the perfect place to learn how people act toward one another. The father let his son go off alone in order to let him see everything and ask questions. The young prince was dressed in beautiful clothing and wore many rings. He was noticed by a poor man who had become a thief. The thief saw an opportunity and offered to guide the young man through the city. He led him to his own house instead and there kept him as a prisoner.

When a few hours passed and the young prince had not returned, the father became worried. He sent out his soldiers to different parts of the town offering a reward of 1000 pieces of gold for the return of his son. The kidnapper heard the offer, but thought he might get even more if he waited another day. The next day at around the same time, the desperate man again heard the soldiers in the street. However, this time the reward was only 500 pieces of gold. He thought he had not heard correctly and decided to wait yet another day. The next day the soldiers passed by once more. However, this time the reward was only 100 pieces of gold. Quickly the man took the boy back to his father.

When the boy was returned and the man had gotten his money, he asked the father why the reward had gotten smaller each day. "The first day my son was angry and refused all your offers of food, did he not?"

"Yes," said the man.

"On the second day, he took your offer of bread, and on the third day he asked you for food?"

"Yes, that is just what happened."

"Well, on the first day he was still a prince. He could still be a great ruler. However, on the second day he had become just like other people. If he became the ruler, he and his people would have to rule together. But by today, he begged for food just like any hungry person would. He was no longer worth anything to me as a ruler but only as my son. Were he ever to rule, he would be overthrown by others and would serve them."

HANDOUT FOR CLASS #22

1. You have been in a Touchstones discussion class for some time now. Pick one new thing you had to learn so that you could help make good discussions. Put down a check if you have learned to do it in class. If you've also begun to do it outside of class, such as at home, underline the sentence too.

    ☐ Listen carefully.
    ☐ Give reasons for what I think.
    ☐ Ask questions that might not have easy answers.
    ☐ Think about other people's ideas.
    ☐ Stop interrupting people when they are talking.
    ☐ Help other people get into the discussion.
    ☐ Not expect an adult to tell me all the answers.

2. Something I've learned that's not on this list.

    _____
    _____

ACTIVITIES FOR CLASS #22

1. Ask the students sit in a circle. Pass out the handout. Have them answer questions #1 and #2 individually. This exercise encourages them to reflect on the Touchstones experience, so give them plenty of time.

2. Have them form small groups of 4-5 to discuss their answers to #1 and #2. There may be some disagreement, but ask them to make a list of 1 or 2 things that everyone agrees they have learned since being in the class, and consider whether they feel any of these skills have carried over into their private roles outside of school.

3. Have students return to the large circle so that each group can report on the items they listed. Make a list on the blackboard or in some other way so that everyone can see. After all groups have reported, ask if they can identify 1 or 2 that have been the hardest to learn.

4. Read the story aloud and have them read it silently. Begin the discussion by asking why the father would pay less money to have his son back. You might also ask them to imagine what things someone would have to learn in order to be a good ruler and how they would have to change.

(These times are approximate only)

1. Sit in circle; answer questions # 1 and #2	8 mins.
2. Small-group work	10 mins.
3. Large-group list of skills learned	8 mins.
4. Read story and discuss	14 mins.
	40 mins.

Class #23   *IMAGES OF WAVES:*
                   The Much Resounding Sea,
                      by Thomas Moran
                   Waves at Matsushima,
                      by Sotatsu

Summary/Purpose:

Lesson #13 of this volume confronted the students with three versions of the same scene. The scene common to the three perspectives was an eagle perched on a cliff who then swoops down to the sea below. The three perspectives involved were different ways of using language. None of them was right or wrong, but each had different advantages and disadvantages depending on the purpose and situation at hand.

This lesson has a similar function except that it involves pictures. The common element is the use of waves, great rolling, crashing waves in both pictures. What is different are the two highly contrasting forms of presentation. The painting by Thomas Moran is realistic, not unlike a skillfully taken photograph. It shows us waves as we imagine we would see them if we visited the seashore on a blustery day. The one by Sotatsu, gold and color on a large folding screen (which accounts for the vertical lines on the accompanying photograph), depicts highly stylized waves with swirls and finger-like edges. No one has ever seen waves quite like these, yet they are unmistakably waves. If we use our imagination, we could say they are more like waves than waves themselves. The wrong question for this lesson is to ask simply "Which is better?" There is no answer to this question if it is asked without context. Yet that question will lurk behind much of the discussion. However, in order for the discussion to be useful and meaningful, it should focus on supplying differing contexts so that the advantages and disadvantages of each perspective can become clear.

The handout asks the students to compare feature-length cartoons and movies to decide which is appropriate under different conditions. For example, what are the pros and cons of using cartoons such as *Aladdin* or *The Lion King* as opposed to regular movies to tell similar stories? In small groups, they should first share their answers to the handouts and then discuss and list what cartoons and movies do best. They should report these lists in the large-group discussion so that you can create a master list for them. If you have time and the resources, you could show them humorous drawings of a politician, an entertainer, or sports figure and compare those with their photographs. (You may wish to bring in a suitable drawing from a newspaper or magazine to help them.) What do caricatures do that photographs can't?

Finally, in the large-group discussion, let them look at the two "Waves" pictures and invite comparisons. Essentially, the questions become what can one picture do that the other can't? and what does each artist have to sacrifice to get the effects he wants? The class should consider whether the finger-like shapes at the tips of the waves on the Japanese screen are more or less like waves than the spray and foam of the Moran painting. As they explore the differences between the paintings, they might reconsider the differences between cartoons and movies. Movies with live actors share certain similarities with the Moran painting. They are similar to what we might experience in real life but are created by a writer with a definite script. The Japanese painting, like the animated feature, is highly imaginative and even exaggerates certain features for us to notice that we might not ordinarily see, such as the tips of the waves.

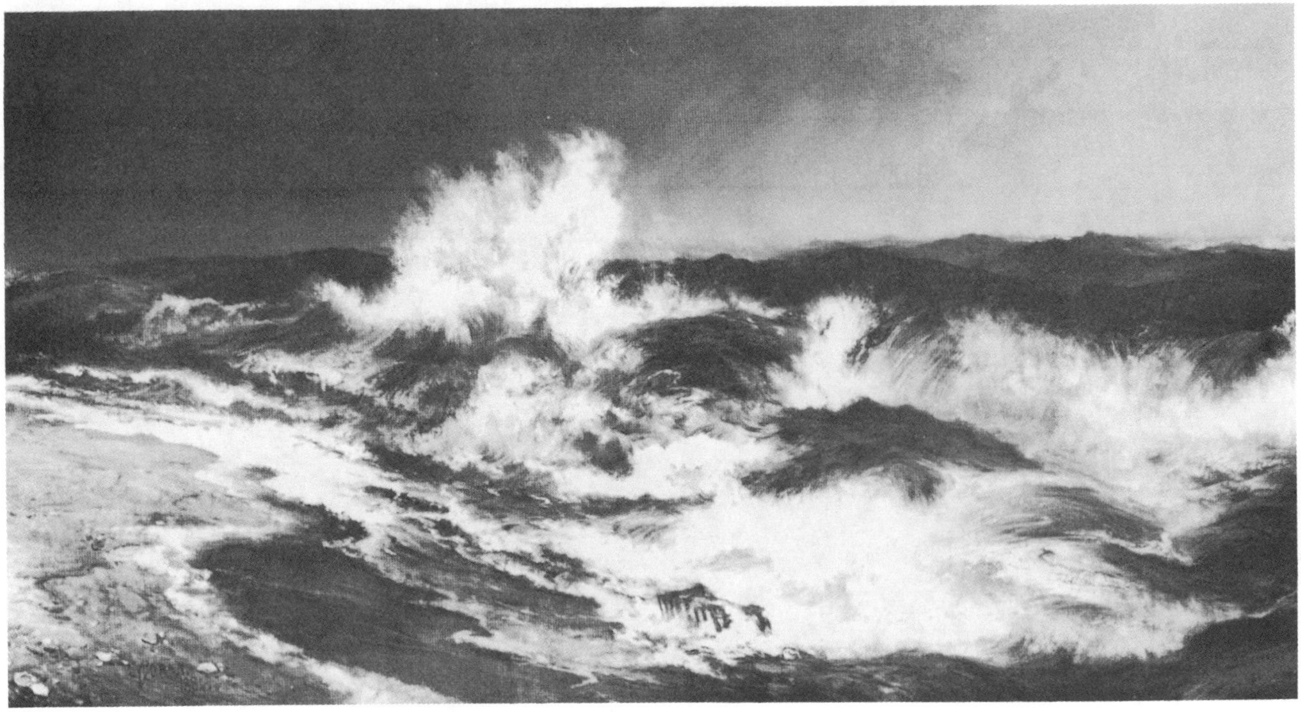

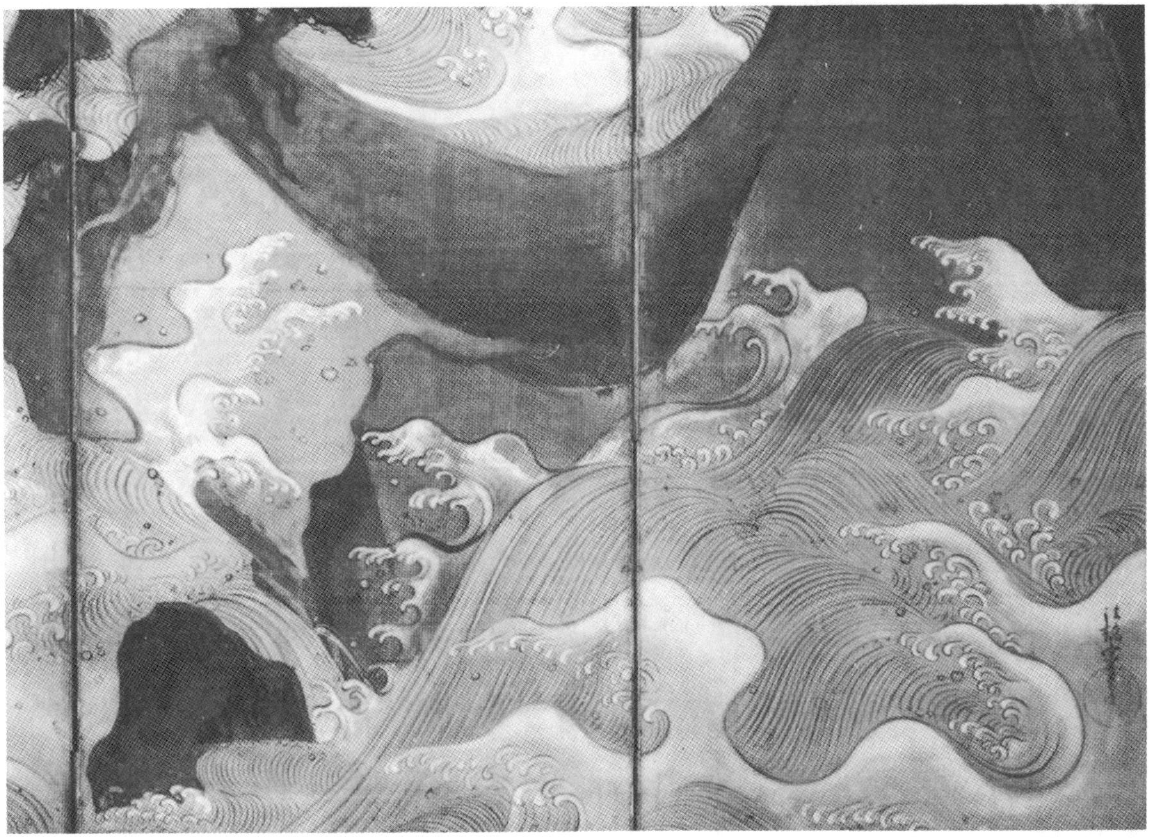

IMAGES OF WAVES:
The Much Resounding Sea, (Student vol., p. 57)
by Thomas Moran
Waves at Matsushima,
by Sotatsu

HANDOUT FOR CLASS #23

1. If you wanted to make a movie of the story of the Prince's kidnapped son (text #22), would it be better to do it as a

    ☐ Movie with real people?   ☐ Animated cartoon?

2. If you wanted to make a movie about how bears live (how they fish, eat, sleep, play, grow up, etc.), would it be better to do it as a

    ☐ Movie with real animals?   ☐ Animated cartoon?

3. If you wanted to make a movie of the story of the lion and the mouse (text #5), would it be better to do it as a

    ☐ Movie with real animals?   ☐ Animated cartoon?

4. If you wanted to make a movie about your family so that people would know how you really live, would you do it as a

    ☐ Movie with real people?   ☐ Animated cartoon?

For each of these questions, be ready to give a good reason for your choice.

ACTIVITIES FOR CLASS #23

1. Ask the students to sit in a circle. Pass out the handout. Have them answer all the questions. Remind them to think of reasons for each answer.

2. Divide them into small groups of 4-5 and ask them to compare their answers to the questions. Then ask them to discuss and make a list of what animated cartoons (like *Aladdin* or *The Lion King*) are best for and what movies with live actors are best for.

   Note: If you have the time, you could also display caricatures or drawings of famous people alongside their photographs. Ask the students to list differences and ask whether photos are always better. What can caricatures do that photos can't?

3. When they have discussed this topic for a few minutes, bring them back into the large group. Have the small groups report on what kinds of things movies do best and when it's better to use a cartoon. Copy the list for each on the blackboard.

4. Show the students the paintings. Tell them that both pictures show waves. How are they both good pictures of waves?

(These times are approximate only)

1. Form circle; answer handout questions	5 mins.
2. Small-group work and discussion	10 mins.
3. List difference between movies and cartoons	10 mins.
4. Show the pictures of waves and discuss	<u>15 mins.</u>
	40 mins.

Class #24   *About Lying,*
                                     by **Montaigne**

Summary/Purpose:

During this year your students have experienced many dimensions of language with which they were previously unfamiliar. In the Touchstones lessons, they have probably begun to sense both the power of language and the problems it can cause.

Through the year they have seen in various ways that *what* was said, and *how* it was said, and *when* it was said are equally important. Sometimes what was said was not understood because a student couldn't state a thought clearly. Sometimes what students said wasn't understood because the words were not known to the other students or because they were used improperly. In these cases communication broke down and an effort had to be made to find different words or expressions which would allow a thought or idea to be understood. In addition, how students said things had a decisive effect. The tone of voice, which words were chosen, and which were stressed made all the difference in whether what students said encouraged discussion or made it temporarily impossible. Finally, when students spoke mattered a great deal: either students said things the class was not ready to hear or things the class was finished with.

Increasingly the students will recognize that words hold us together as human beings but can also keep us apart. Language makes it possible for us to experience the most precious emotions of friendship and love as well as the harshest feelings of anger and hatred. Language makes cooperation possible and brings complex societies into existence, but it can also tear us into factions and create sustained conflict and war. Language is so deeply part of what we are that it is perhaps impossible to imagine a human being without language. In today's class, they will look at this extraordinary tool, language.

Some scientists and thinkers have suggested that language is not the special possession of human beings. In fact, they have explored indications of language among animals, insects, and birds. It would be useful at some point to encourage your students to discuss whether they think animals such as dogs and cats possess language and what they believe animals are capable of doing with the sounds they make. However, in spite of these various theories about animal languages, no one has seriously suggested that animals are capable of a very peculiar linguistic act: lying. Telling a lie is a very complex activity which, as we and your students know all too well, happens quite frequently among us. Someone who lies is not just making a mistake. Rather, a liar deliberately presents a set of words as true when in fact the liar knows or believes they are not true. Part of telling a lie therefore involves recognizing the difference between what is true and what is false. Saying things which are true is the most important way we use language. It is what we normally expect. But there is always the possibility that language can be used to tell a lie. This difference makes it possible to consider language itself.

The text by Montaigne will enable the students to discuss these issues as well as others. Montaigne first contends that lying successfully is very difficult. If the lie is entirely made up, it's hard to remember. If, on the other hand, the lie is close to the truth, then frequently liars get mixed up in the truth. In addition, if people discover you are good at lying, then of course lying becomes more difficult. All these points about the difficulty of lying as well as the fact that a liar cannot take credit for telling lies may well be aimed at convincing people not to lie. This is because Montaigne believes that lying is one of the most serious dangers human beings confront. He claims that words are what hold us together and that lying threatens these bonds. He therefore believes that children should be most seriously punished for lying. It is a habit that, once it develops, is extremely difficult to break. These are issues you should encourage your students to consider. Though Montaigne's text specifically deals with lying, you should view this as one of the ways in which language, though it leads to our most valuable and important activities, brings great risks with it. Language can be used to encourage people and make them feel good about things but also to discourage them and make them lose confidence. You should encourage the class to consider other such cases. Your students have had much experience this year in Touchstones of both the positive and negative possibilities of language.

About Lying, (Student vol., p. 59)
by Montaigne

People who lie either completely invent what they say or they change and hide something which is true. In either case, it is very easy to trap them if you ask them many questions. When they lie by changing something which is true, they keep getting mixed up by the truth. For what they know is true is more firmly in their minds than the lie that is so similar to it. The truth therefore keeps getting in the way. In cases where they make up the whole story, it is hard for them to remember what they said. This is because there is nothing else in their minds that is similar to the lie.

Sometimes people are admired because they are good at lying. These people use words to please others and say what they think people wish to hear. But since people are so different, they must lie in different ways to different people. They tell one person that something is gray and another that it is yellow. But what happens if these people talk to each other about what the liar said? Also, it is hard to lie because if people know that you do it, they won't believe you. So if you're admired for your ability to lie, you will no longer be able to do it, since everyone knows you lie.

Lying is a very bad thing. We humans are held together only by our words. If we realized how bad lying is, we would punish it more than almost any other crime. It is silly that people often punish harmless faults in children. Only lying should get the worst punishment. Unlike most other faults, it grows with the child. Once children have started to lie, it is very difficult to change them.

HANDOUT FOR CLASS #24

Check the sentences below that you think are lies.

☐   Bob asks Joe how to get somewhere and Joe tells him he thinks it's that way. Later Joe discovers it was another way.

☐   Bill asks Mary if she likes what he is wearing, and Mary says "yes" even though she doesn't.

☐   A bully asks John where John's best friend is. John knows but says he doesn't.

☐   Mr. Smith catches Francis looking at Pat's test paper, but Francis denies it.

☐   In a discussion, Sue repeats what other people have said instead of saying what she thinks.

☐   Eric broke a school window with a rock and David saw him do it, but doesn't say anything to anyone.

☐   Tom broke a friend's favorite toy but says he didn't do it.

☐   Cathy is having trouble in school. Mrs. Jones, the teacher, tells her that she will succeed if she studies hard.

ACTIVITIES FOR CLASS #24

1. Ask the students to sit in a circle. Pass out the handout. Have students answer the question individually.

2. Break the class into small groups of 4-5 and have them share their answers. There will be disagreement over the gray areas. Ask them to decide which is the worst lie and why, and which is most clearly not a lie and why.

3. Bring the students back into the large circle and ask them to report on what they agreed was the worst lie and what wasn't. Ask them to tell the class clearly why they made their decisions. Discussion may well begin, especially in trying to assess the reasons. This is fine, but make sure each group gets a chance to report.

4. Read the text and ask your students whether they agree that we humans are held together by words. Ask also whether they think that animals have language and if so what they talk about. Finally, ask them if they agree that lying is as bad as Montaigne says it is and whether they have any other reasons why lying is bad.

(These times are approximate only)

1. Sit in circle; answer the handout.	5 mins.
2. Small-group work	10 mins.
3. Large group; small-group reports	10 mins.
4. Read text and discuss	<u>15 mins.</u>
	40 mins.

Class #25 *The Man Who Thought He Could Do Anything,*
A Tale of Native America

Summary/Purpose:

Students are often tempted to make learning a purely individual challenge and accomplishment, something they do on their own. Schools often reinforce this in assigning grades, for students consider grades a mark of individual effort and accomplishment. Thus it becomes especially easy for bright students to believe that they must learn only by themselves. Students who don't do well may also believe they cannot ask their classmates for help even though it is not possible to do everything oneself. This will be especially true when your students eventually enter the work force. Yet, in the early years of the industrial revolution, a high degree of individual specialization was thought to be the best approach to manufacturing and even to intellectual research and scholarship. Although such an approach involved an extremely complex interdependence among workers, each worker had a solitary and very precise task to master. It therefore did not require real skills of cooperation. The factory assembly line is the model of such organization.

Over the last 30 years, as computers and technology have advanced, this previous model has become obsolete. People now need to learn how to cooperate with others who have very different skills and backgrounds. Any real problem or task requires input from a variety of people from different professions. The danger in the purely traditional forms of education is that students often become convinced they must "do it alone." If that idea takes hold, students may begin to define "everything" as the things they do well and so believe that what they don't do well is not really worth doing. They probably originally had doubts about a process like Touchstones, one goal of which is collaboration, a sharing of strengths for the benefit of all. Discussion is something no one can do alone, a fact about discussion that applies to many other types of learning as well. Touchstones complements the regular curriculum. In regular classes students master specific skills. In Touchstones they learn to respect people with different skills and to practice how to cooperate. They need this additional skill in order adequately to utilize the specific skills they will learn. If they believe they must do everything alone, they will accomplish very little. This week's story raises these issues by describing a person who feels a great need to do everything alone.

Manabozho is a powerful wizard who is consumed by pride. His pride is built on his confident belief that he can do anything. In the story he tries to do what he sees a baby do. Because his body is no longer as flexible as the baby's is, he fails. His trying to do what a baby does easily and naturally will probably strike your students as silly, as indeed it is. But the desire to do everything does lead to absurdities and an inability to distinguish between what one must do alone or with others, and between what is worth doing or what is a waste of time. It can also lead to despair: how am I ever going to learn this? Manabozho feels this despair. He has set such a strange and high standard for himself that failure even in this one small activity causes him to doubt his other abilities. It also makes him lash out at others, as if they were at fault. He discharges his anger by turning an innocent boy into a tree. Students must explore for themselves when it is appropriate to do something oneself and when it is better to seek help. Every learner knows that there is too much to learn and certainly far too much to learn by oneself. The discussion may also raise the question of what the role of the teacher is as well. Should the teacher be expected to know all the answers? What is the purpose of education in general? Is it to learn everything there is? If not, what is the goal? Some people claim it is to learn how to learn, but what does that mean?

As a teacher, you are probably enthusiastic about the real benefits of cooperative learning. Your students will now have an opportunity to understand cooperation a little better, even as they are being trained by the demands of the discussion method to be able to do it. The handout will help them think about these issues by focusing them on what they think is better to learn alone or with the help of others. The Activities page suggests that you ask the students what difference it would make to the discussion class if a teacher were to grade everyone.

The Man Who Thought He Could Do Anything, (Student vol., p. 61)
A Tale of Native America

Manabozho was a great and powerful wizard. He went from tribe to tribe doing many great deeds and was looked up to by everyone. He became so powerful that he began to think he could do anything. His deeds were wonderful and everyday he grew more and more proud of himself. He expected everyone to treat him with great respect, and he looked down on those who were not as strong or smart as he was. One day while walking through the forest feeling good about himself, he came to a campsite. There he saw a young child lying in the sunshine. The child was curled up resting and had its toe in its mouth.

The wizard Manabozho was amazed. He looked with great wonder at how the child was lying on the ground. "I've never seen a child do that before. But if a child can do it, I'm sure I can do it too." So he lay down beside the child to imitate him and put his body just as the child had his. He took his right foot in his hand and moved it toward his mouth. But try as hard as he might his foot stayed far from his lips. He tried again with his left foot but found that he failed again. He twisted his body every way he could think of, bent his arms and legs, stretched his neck but couldn't do what the child did. As he was doing this, the little child opened his eyes, released his toe, stretched out, turned over, and in a moment had the toe of his other foot in his mouth. The warm sun made the baby make comforting, cooing sounds as he fell back asleep.

The wizard watched the baby and was very angry. "I cannot do it," he said, rising. "Perhaps all my great power is gone." He heard the cooing sounds and thought the baby was laughing at him. Angry and sad, he thought about taking revenge, but his attention was caught by some noise in the forest. He walked quickly away into the forest and saw a young boy on a path. The boy was not paying any attention and ran into the wizard. Very angry, the wizard said, "Have you no respect for me?" "It was an accident," said the boy. Unhappy and in a rage, the wizard said, "You will never run again," and at that moment the boy was turned into a tree. "At least I can still do something," said the wizard, starting to feel good about himself again.

HANDOUT FOR CLASS #25

Some of the things below it may be best to learn by yourself; for some of them it may be best to get some kind of help from others. Check the box that is the best answer for you.

	by myself	Some kind of help from others
a. Learning to play tennis	☐	☐
b. Learning to run long distances	☐	☐
c. Learning to draw pictures	☐	☐
d. Learning to cook	☐	☐
e. Learning to fish	☐	☐
f. Learning to ride a bike	☐	☐
g. Learning arithmetic	☐	☐
h. Learning to shoot a basketball	☐	☐
i. Memorizing a list of important dates	☐	☐
j. Practicing an instrument	☐	☐
k. Learning to write neatly	☐	☐

ACTIVITIES FOR CLASS #25

1. Ask the students to sit in a circle. Pass out the handout. Have them fill out answers to the question individually.

2. Break the class into small groups of 4-5 and have them share their answers. If there is disagreement, let them provide and explore reasons why the item is best learned all by oneself or with some kind of help from others.

3. Ask all the students to form the large circle again. Tell them that the Touchstones discussion classes are not graded, but if a teacher wanted to grade the students, how do they imagine it could be done? What effect would grades have on Touchstones discussions?

4. Read the story and begin the discussion by asking them why Manabozho felt he had to do just what the baby did or why turning the boy into a tree made him feel better. If the discussion becomes too abstract or textual, ask the class whether someone like Manabozho would like being in a Touchstones discussion class: why or why not?

(These times are approximate only)

1. Sit in circle and answer handout	5 mins.
2. Small-group work	10 mins.
3. Large group: grading discussion	10 mins.
4. Read story and discuss	<u>15 mins.</u>
	40 mins.

Class #26   *Robinson Crusoe,*
                              by Daniel Defoe

Summary/Purpose:

 Most objects in the world or events in our lives have a good side and a bad side. They can appear bad when looked at in one way, or good if cast in a different light. For example, nuclear power can be used to our great advantage or its abuse can cause utter devastation. A person with Alzheimer's disease can be viewed as someone with a terrible illness or as the center of a family acting in loving cooperation. This particular instance of the possibility of dual perspectives might be new to your students. Most of the cases we have considered this year involved trying to view something as it would be seen by someone else. This situation is different. The students are asked to consider a situation and draw two sets of consequences, one which they feel is good, the other bad. Most of the decisions they will make in their lives are of this form, especially in whatever jobs they will eventually hold. There are always pluses and minuses to decisions and what we eventually decide to do involves a sort of calculation about what is better or worse rather than what is simply good or bad. This lesson therefore begins to give them practice in evaluating evidence and consequences, and in decision-making.

 The text for today is from an early part of the story of Robinson Crusoe's life on an island. Crusoe's ship sinks and he washes up on shore. He is alone and begins a survey of things useful for his survival. After taking care of the immediate needs he has for a hut, some food, and fire, he makes two lists; on one side he lists the good aspects of his life, on the other side the bad. He arranges the list so that the *same feature* of his life can be viewed as either good or bad, depending on what he emphasizes. In the text for the students, we have completed only two features: having no clothes and being alone. Having no clothes can be seen as embarrassing and uncomfortable and hence a bad thing, or it can be seen as good, since he is alone and the weather is always warm. Secondly, being alone can be bad if you emphasize the lack of friendship, but it can be good if you realize that at least you don't have anyone with whom to argue and disagree. Robinson Crusoe's list goes on for many more items, but our text purposely breaks off after two and part of the third. It points out that it is bad not to have friends, and, because the text breaks off there, invites the students to find some perspective to make that same feature appear good.

The handout asks the students to continue the list on their own, adding a "good" for each "bad" that is given. Then, in small groups they are asked to do one more task: they must try to find both a "good" and a "bad" that they think can stand on their own. That is, they must find one event or thing which they can decide is good or bad but for which they can *not* think of a corresponding good or bad: this involves trying to decide if something is wholly good or wholly bad.

In the class discussion, ask the groups to report their unqualifiedly "good" or "bad" things. Then ask the class to propose a perspective from which the good could seem bad, and vice versa. Some might come easily, others will be hard. The group might well decide that some things are indeed always good or bad. Put the difficult ones on the board to consider later, and move on to other small-group reports.

If there is time in the later part of this class period, ask their reaction to the second part of the text. Would they be excited and glad that they found a fresh footprint in the sand, or would they become more and more worried and frightened as Robinson Crusoe did?

Robinson Crusoe,   (Student vol., p. 63)
by Daniel Defoe

On September 30th, 1659, I, poor, unhappy Robinson Crusoe, was shipwrecked during a dreadful storm, and came to shore on this bare island, which I named the "Island of Despair." All others on my ship were drowned, and I was washed up almost dead. Over the next few days, several useful things were washed ashore from the destroyed ship, such as some tools, planks of wood, corn seeds, salted meat, and even a large chest of money. I smiled to myself as I thought how useless all that money was to me now.

With great difficulty and pain, I made myself a hut, planted the corn, and generally began doing daily jobs to help me survive. I continued this hard life for a year, at the end of which I made two lists. On one side, I wrote all the things which in this life alone on the island I called Bad; on the other side, I listed the Good.

Here is the beginning of my list:

Bad	**Good**
I have no clothes to cover me, but	this island is in a warm part of the world, so I don't need any.
I am alone and have no one to speak to, but	at least no one ever argues or disagrees with me.
I have no friends here, but . . .	

After many, many months, I was walking one day towards the little boat I had built, when I was very surprised and shocked to see the print of a man's naked foot in the sand by the shore. I stood still like a statue, as if I had seen a ghost. I listened and looked around me but I could neither hear nor see anything. I walked the beach, but found no more footprints. I even went up in the hills, but saw no one who could have made that footprint.

My heart beat faster as I went back to my hut, looking behind me at every two or three steps, looking behind bushes and up trees. I soon began to run to my castle (for so I pretended it to be now) and stayed there, too frightened to leave it. That night I did not sleep at all. In fact, the longer the time since I first saw the footprint, the more afraid I became. I kept thinking I saw a person when there was no one.

HANDOUT FOR CLASS #26

To Be Completed by You Alone

1. Robinson Crusoe begins a list of bad and good ways of looking at parts of his life alone on the island. The first two he has completed. You are to complete the next two as Robinson Crusoe did; that is, make up a way of looking at these two apparently bad things that shows that they can also be seen as good.

Bad	**Good**
I have no clothes to cover me, but . . .	this island is in a warm part of the world, so I don't need any.
I am alone and have no one to speak to, but . . .	at least no one ever argues or disagrees with me.
I have no friends here, but . . .	_____
Many things that I like to eat I can't find or buy here, but . . .	_____

To Be Completed in the Small Groups

2. Write one thing that you all think is just good, so good that you cannot think of any way it could be seen as bad. Also think of one thing which seems always bad.

Only Good:

Only Bad:

133

ACTIVITIES FOR CLASS #26

1. Ask your students to sit in a circle and read them the story, having them read it silently. You should emphasize the list, making it clear to them that Robinson Crusoe is looking at the same thing from two sides or viewpoints.

2. Pass out the handout and have them answer question #1 on their own.

3. Break them into pairs (one group of three if needed) and have them tell each other what "goods" they added to Crusoe's list. Then have them work together to answer question #2.

4. Have the students come back to the circle and let each group report their always "good" and "bad" things. Ask the class to think of comments so that perhaps some of these apparently "good" or "bad" things can be seen in the opposite light. List the hard ones on the board and consider them later, but don't force the students to find a negative or positive viewpoint if they don't want to.

5. Discuss Crusoe's finding of the footprint and how the students would feel in his place.

(These times are approximate only)

1. Sit in circle; read story	5 mins.
2. Individual work on handout	5 mins.
3. Pairs; answer question #2	10 mins.
4. Form large circle and report list of unqualifiedly "good" or "bad" things and discuss possible opposites.	10 mins.
5. Discuss finding the footprint	<u>10 mins.</u>
	40 mins.

Class #27   *Narcissus,*
                                    A Story from Greece

Summary/Purpose:

The entire year has been devoted to the creation of complex skills that will enable your students to improve their learning. Undoubtedly they have developed discussion skills individually and as a group. But other skills which emerge in a discussion environment are equally important. These skills will transfer to regular classes and enable students to gain more from your teaching. Central among these skills is the ability to listen. Listening is an active skill, though we often think of it as passive. Many people have difficulty listening, but not because they have not heard the words that were uttered. Rather, listening is difficult because we generally hear what we want to hear. In other words, we tend to hear what we already believe; we hear ourselves rather than what another person is really saying.

This becomes a crucial problem in learning because often what we *need* to learn either conflicts or only distantly connects with what we already know and feel confident about. For instance, when people believed the sun went around the earth, they often refused to listen to arguments that the earth went around the sun. In the same way, how do we teach arithmetic to someone who is good at language arts but is afraid of numbers? How do we build on what that student can already do? As we teachers well know, such situations present various problems in our classes and must be approached carefully. It therefore becomes imperative that students learn to cooperate with us by listening actively to what we are saying or what a text is presenting, and not to what they wish to hear or expect to hear. Not to be able to listen accurately will mean that students will not be able to undertake serious intellectual change. They will not be able to respond to the ever-increasing demands placed on them by new information, approaches, skills, and theories. Whether they realize it or not, they will remain captive within themselves, attached to their own reflections.

This week's text presents the story of someone literally in this situation, Narcissus. The myth of Narcissus is the story of someone who fell in love with his own reflection. Narcissus was very good looking and many fell in love with him. However, he preferred his own company and kept himself apart from others. One day, tired from hunting, he wished to refresh himself at a clear lake. When he did, he saw a very attractive face looking back at him. According to the myth, Narcissus fell in love with this face staring back at him in the water, never realizing that this face was his own. Captivated by his own reflection, he was held immobile and eventually wasted away. This story is therefore the image of the very situation described above. It is an image of those who do not listen. Therefore, in considering this story, the students will face the same problem that confronted Narcissus. He must recognize that the face in the water he loves is just the reflection of his own face. They must recognize how this can be a story about themselves. You might start the discussion by asking them how Narcissus could have figured out that the face was his own and follow it up by asking their opinions on what he would have done if he had figured that out: would he have remained there or gotten up and left?

This consideration of the text should come first in this week's class, before they do the handout. After about 10 minutes of discussion, have them complete the handout. The handout has them consider other situations that are similar to the story and decide which case is most like the case of Narcissus. One of them is the issue of hearing and listening. You should have them explore that after they complete the handout (See Activities, #4). Learning how to listen will take years to master; this week's class raises the issue to be talked about. However, participating in the Touchstones discussions themselves will enable students to practice this skill concretely.

Narcissus, (Student vol., p. 67)
A Story from Greece

Even as a little boy, Narcissus was very good looking. As he grew older, he grew even more handsome. By the time he was sixteen, he was so handsome that people fell in love with him just by looking at him. But he didn't want anything to do with anyone else; he just wanted to be by himself.

Once he was hunting in the forest when a lovely girl, whose name was Echo, saw him and fell in love at first sight. For a while, she only followed him around, but soon she came up to throw her arms around him and hold him. But Narcissus ran away from her and cried out, "Take your hands off me. Don't touch me. I'd rather die than have your hands on me."

Echo was so sad and unhappy that she called after him. "One day I hope *you* fall in love with someone like I have with you. You'll feel how awful it is when someone doesn't love you back."

One day soon after, Narcissus became tired after hunting in the forest, and came upon a beautiful lake surrounded by flowers and trees. No one had ever been in that part of the forest before. Narcissus was hot and thirsty, so he laid himself down by the lake and leaned over the edge to take a drink of water. At once he saw a face in the water, which was just like a mirror.

As soon as he saw the face, he stopped still, staring at it. He saw how good looking it was, and soon fell deeply in love. He was so much in love that he couldn't take his eyes off the face in the water. All he knew was that if he moved at all, then the face also moved. It never occurred to him that he was in love with his own face. So he continued to lie very still, loving the face, until he wasted away, because he would neither eat nor drink. Thus he died.

HANDOUT FOR CLASS #27

1. Some of the following people might be just like Narcissus, in love with themselves and not even knowing it. Which person is the *most* like Narcissus? Circle the person's name.

    a. John only likes people who think as he does.

    b. Mary only plays with people who dress and look like her.

    c. When James listens to you, he only really pays attention to what he agrees with.

    d. Jack is always very worried over whether people like him.

    e. Susan only wants her friends to say nice things to her.

2. Why do you think the person you picked is most like Narcissus? Think of a good reason.

ACTIVITIES FOR CLASS #27

1. Ask the students to sit in a circle. Read the story and begin by clearing up any details they don't understand. Then ask them how Narcissus could have figured out that he was really looking at his own face.

2. After 10 minutes of discussion, pass out the handout and ask them to answer the questions individually. Make sure they understand that they are to circle the name of the person most like Narcissus and that they should think of a good reason for their choice.

3. Divide them into small groups of 4-5 and have them share their answers. See if it is possible for them to agree which person is the most like Narcissus.

4. Have the students return to the large circle and ask the small groups to report. After they have reported, explore the issue of listening with them. Ask them what they think good listening requires and what they think they can do to learn to listen more accurately.

(These times are approximate only)

1. Form circle; read story and discuss	10 mins.
2. Answer handout individually	5 mins.
3. Small-group work	10 mins.
4. Large group convenes: Small-group reports, discuss listening	<u>15 mins.</u>
	40 mins.

Class #28 *The Spider and the Turtle,*
A Tale from the Ashanti People of Africa

Summary/Purpose:

We are used to thinking of customs as applying to the way people live in foreign countries, but each home has its own customs and is, in that sense, foreign territory, at least to others. Thus we learn to be prepared when we visit other people's homes to abide by the rules of their house, for we expect that our hosts will do some things differently than we do. Your students will have had this experience when they stay overnight at friends' homes. Customs of the house sometimes require only minor adjustments, like politely eating portions of food we are not used to. But customs may require visitors to make major concessions. For example, students who pray before meals at home may visit friends who pray different prayers or who do not pray at all. In this week's class, the students will begin to explore how differently people can live their lives and therefore how differently they can see the world. This issue will concern us over the next three classes. In this lesson, they will consider the customs of their own families and also the "customs" of the discussion class itself.

This week's story tells how a spider avoided sharing his dinner with a turtle and how the turtle eventually got even. Students may first notice and wish to discuss the clever trickery that goes on in the story, but the occasion for the trickery is custom. Both the spider and the turtle use custom to make their guest feel unwelcome; that is, they use customs to accentuate and even exaggerate the differences between them. Students should spend time discussing how hosts should behave toward guests and how guests should adapt to the customs of the house they are visiting. Should they expect visitors to their homes to adapt to what usually happens there? Should they do things differently so that their friends feel comfortable? Should they think of compromising? You might ask them if a friend came to dinner who didn't eat meat, should they prepare a special meatless meal that everyone could enjoy or let their friend adapt? This is also a good time to reflect on the customs of the Touchstones discussion class itself.

The story presents two very different creatures, a spider and a turtle. The turtle is lost in the forest and very hungry when he smells the delicious aroma of the spider's dinner. Spider law requires the spider to feed the turtle as a guest, but he doesn't really wish to abide by the spirit of that law. So he uses a custom, hand washing, to make it clear that the turtle is not welcome and to ensure that he won't have to share his food. The turtle treats the spider the same way when he visits later, so that the spider feels as the turtle did. It is an open question in the story whether the spider's custom of hand washing or the turtle's of jacket removing are real customs or whether they are made up to prevent real hospitality without seeming overly greedy or revengeful. That is, it might be a way to put the blame on the custom.

The perspectives here are several. Students may well remark on how they themselves behave differently as guests or hosts. For example, as a visiting child's host, they may have had to share even their favorite toys or entertain their guest even when they'd rather play with their neighborhood friends. As guests, they may have had to play games they don't play very much or felt that they always had to do what their host said. Students may use the story to reflect on times when hosts have used customs that made them feel either welcome or unwelcome. Finally, they may reflect generally on how customs seem necessary in order to be able to have discussions: every member of the group must submit in some degree to the external rules that make discussion possible. You may use this opportunity to ask them how well they are doing at keeping these customs of the class and whether the customs ever prevent people from having a part to play in the discussion.

The Spider and the Turtle, (Student vol., p. 67)
A Tale from the Ashanti People of Africa

It was nearly dark when the turtle found a clearing in the woods and rested. There was a wonderful smell of cooked fish and fresh fruit. He followed the smell and found the spider about to eat his dinner. The spider was unhappy to see the turtle because he didn't want to share his food. However, spiders have a law never to refuse food to a stranger. So he invited the turtle in, and the tired turtle felt happy about his good luck. Just as the turtle was about to put food in his mouth, the spider said in a stern voice, "Turtle, in my country we always wash before eating. Please go to the stream and wash your paws. I see dust on them from your trip." The turtle wished to be a good guest and did as he was told. But when he returned, the spider had already eaten half the food. As the turtle tried to pick up some fish, the spider jumped across the table. "You call that washed?" he said, pointing to some dirt on the turtle's paws. The turtle felt ashamed and went back to the stream one more time. When he finally returned clean and ready to eat, all the food was gone. The turtle was angry but said, "Thank you for your invitation. Some day you must come and visit me."

A few months later the spider was out walking and hurt himself. For a few days he couldn't move. When he was finally able to walk, he struggled down to the river. There he found the turtle, who said, "Spider, you look terrible." The spider replied, "Yes, I was hurt and haven't eaten in days." The turtle smiled and said, "Well, come to my house at the bottom of the river and I will feed you a wonderful meal." The turtle went deep down into the water to prepare the food and the spider tried to follow. But he couldn't get to the bottom because he was so light. So the clever spider put many pebbles in his coat pockets and tried again. This time he sank down to the turtle's house. There he saw the most wonderful food he had ever seen. Excited by his good luck, he sat down and the turtle handed him a full plate. But, just as he was to take a bite, the turtle said, "Spider, in my country we never wear a coat to dinner. Please take off your coat." Very slowly the spider removed his coat. As he did, he began to rise in the water away from the table. Without the pebbles, he floated up to the surface as he watched all that wonderful food eaten up by the turtle.

The moral is, when you try to trick someone for selfish reasons, there is always someone trickier than you.

HANDOUT FOR CLASS #28

1. Every family has its own customs, ways of doing things that stay the same and that guests have to get used to. We notice our customs best at holidays like Thanksgiving when we eat special foods and do special things together. Pick your favorite holiday and think of some of the special things your family does. The questions are to help you with your answer. You can write answers down if you wish.

    a. What holiday is your favorite?

    b. If you get to eat special foods, which do you like best?

    c. Do you do any special activities together? What is one?

    d. What is one thing your family always tries to do together on that holiday?

Do not answer #2 until your teacher tells you to.

2. What are the customs in the Touchstones class (the things you expect yourself and everyone to do, and that you all succeed in doing)? Check the boxes with ✓. Help your teacher make a list.

    ☐ Never raise hands
    ☐ Interrupt people when we want to talk
    ☐ Listen with respect
    ☐ Help others get into the discussion
    ☐ Laugh when someone says something silly
    (You write down one more)

ACTIVITIES FOR CLASS #28

1. Ask the students to sit in a circle. Pass out the handout. Have them think of (or jot down) some answers to question #1. Do not deal with question #2 yet. The purpose at this stage is to help define what a custom is and provide material for them to share with each other. It may be a revelation to some children, for example, to hear how differently other children celebrate important holidays, for they generally assume that all families are like their own.

2. Ask the class to break into small groups and discuss their answers to question #1. Give them plenty of time to explore and enjoy their differences.

3. Ask them to come back to the large group and read the story to them, asking them to read silently. Begin the discussion by asking them how the spider could have made the turtle feel welcome. Students will probably say that the spider should have let the turtle eat, but ask them about the hand washing. Does this seem like a good custom or a bad custom? How could the turtle and spider make each other welcome in each other's homes in the future despite being so different and despite having tricked each other once before?

4. After about 10 minutes, ask them to complete question #2. Have volunteers tell their answers about the additional customs to begin with. Write down the customs on the board and allow some discussion about whether these are in fact the customs of this group. There are general customs for the Touchstones class (no hand raising), but your class may have developed its own particular customs.

5. End by asking them what they would do to make a visiting child feel welcome in their Touchstones class.

(These times are approximate only)

1. Sit in circle; handout #1	5 mins.
2. Small-group work	10 mins.
3. Read story and discuss	10 mins.
4. Complete question #2; list and discuss Touchstones customs	7 mins.
5. Hospitality discussion	<u>8 mins.</u>
	40 mins.

Class #29 *THE COVER MAP OF ICELAND*

Summary/Purpose:

One of the crucial skills emerging from participation in Touchstones is decision-making. This occurs both in the intellectual and behavioral realms. Your students have now had much experience in discussing topics, working in small groups, and in completing the handouts to choose approaches, ideas, or strategies. Now, near the end of the year, it is appropriate to make this subject explicit. This will be done in this lesson by considering how to make a map and how to read it.

Making a map involves making very clear choices. First, what is the purpose of the map? Suppose we consider a map of the U.S.A., less Alaska and Hawaii. Not everything can be given equal value. Some features will be stressed, some played down, many completely ignored. Is the purpose of the map to reveal political differences? If so, it will outline the state borders, or the county lines, or the voting constituency borders. Is the map's function to show topographical differences? If so, it may ignore the states and counties in order to stress elevation contour lines, even to the point of having many shades of brown and green. A map used to navigate a river will be radically different from a highly detailed street map of a city. Even the outline of the whole country, or of a state or county, will change depending on whether one wants to represent the road system (in which case the outline might be schematized as simple straight lines at angles), or whether one wishes to have the size of each state represent the differences in population (in which case Rhode Island would be drawn half the size of Utah, and California sixteen times larger than Utah). Using a map requires learning how to read it. It involves recognizing the perspective from which the map is drawn.

The text for this lesson is the cover map of *Touchpebbles: Volume A*. It is an early map of Iceland, and they will spend the first minutes of the class "reading" it with a great deal of help from you. With the whole class sitting in their usual circle, ask them to try to say what seems important to the person who drew this map. Which is the most mountainous part of the country? Tell them there are live volcanoes on Iceland. Where are they? Where might the farming be good? There are no trees in the country, but valuable tree logs drift in on the eastern coast. Important churches and monasteries are marked with a †. Where are they? If they landed in Iceland and had no way of going away again, where might they settle? Why?

For your information, the map presents other interesting features. Mountains are signified by round elevations (even though the actual mountains are jagged) and the word "Jokul." Only major mountains are marked. "Hekla" the volcano is depicted emitting fire and smoke as well as rocks. It was often the first thing sailors could see because they approached from the southeast. Various pictures of animals show where good pasturing or hunting could be found. Although hard to see, small birds perch on cliffs below Hekla. They are hawks and falcons, valuable to train as hunters and for the medieval sport of falconry. The various sea creatures are part fanciful and part realistic: some are whales, others are fish good to eat. The dotted line in the middle divides two church dioceses. Note that there are no trails or roads depicted. Finally, in the northeast the mapmaker depicts ice floes with polar bears on them, very dangerous to unwary hunters. If possible, you may want to show pictures of Iceland or at least a modern map. Those who discovered Iceland gave it that name to discourage settlers, for they considered it a very good place to live.

The handout for this lesson will ask the students to draw a map. They are to deal with a very specific task, how a friend should go the last few blocks or the final distance to visit them at home. They are to put certain features as landmarks on the map which their friend should look for, a church, a school, other houses, so they will not get lost. They should also consider how their house is best recognized, for example, whether by its color, distinctive features, street number, or vegetation in front. Also they should take into account how their friend will get there (by car, on foot, by bike) and indicate the best routes for each. They may be the same or different. What else might be a problem or a danger? Is there a fierce dog nearby, a bad hole in the street, etc. This will be presented first in a checklist where they will make decisions on what to represent. After they decide on what features will help, they should then draw a map which incorporates these features. You will probably need to give them a great deal of guidance for this exercise.

When they have completed all these jobs, ask them to break into pairs (or three if needed.) In these pairs they are to try to "read" each other's maps. Finally, after bringing the whole class together again in a circle, the discussion should turn on any difficulties the students encountered in creating the maps and in reading them. In particular you should have them compare reading a map with reading a painting, a story, and a poem.

HANDOUT FOR CLASS #29

A friend is coming to see you at home but has never been there before. You want your friend to have a map so as not to get lost. Check below what you feel your map should have in order to get your friend safely there. For each question below you can check one or more boxes.

A. How will your friend know it's your house?
- ☐ color
- ☐ street number can be seen
- ☐ near certain other houses or buildings,
- ☐ unusual parts of the house such as big driveway, porch, or a large garage with basketball backboard on it.
- ☐ trees or bushes in front

B. How will your friend get there?
- ☐ car, so roads need to be drawn
- ☐ on foot, so walking route needs to be shown
- ☐ bike, so bike path needs to be shown

C. Are there any very big buildings or hills or rivers nearby that your friend will see and know your house is near?
- ☐ churches or schools or large stores
- ☐ hills, river, lake, or some other natural feature.

D. Is there anything your friend should be careful about?
- ☐ big dogs or other animals
- ☐ broken sidewalks or holes in the streets
- ☐ dangerous area

Now, on the back of this paper, draw a map of the area close to your house, perhaps the last two blocks, and put the things you checked above on your map.

ACTIVITIES FOR CLASS #29

1. Ask your students to sit in a circle. Tell them that today's lesson is to look at the map that makes up the cover of their *Touchpebbles: Volume A*. Explain that it is a map of Iceland drawn hundreds of years ago. You may wish to have them locate it on a globe so that they can see how close it is to the North Pole. Ask them to pick out details; help them as you see fit. The Summary/Purpose section of this lesson may be of help to you.

2. Ask the group what seems most important to the person who drew the map. Let discussion continue for about 5 minutes.

3. Pass out the handout and ask them to make their own map. Explain to them the connection between the handout questions and their drawing of the map.

4. Break the students into pairs (or threes) and have them "read" each others maps.

5. Reconvene all the students in a circle and discuss with them what made the exercise difficult. Students may also discuss the cover again.

(These times are approximate only)

1. Form circle; read map and discuss	10 mins.
2. Pass handout; make map	10 mins.
3. Small-group work: reading the maps	8 mins.
4. Large group; discuss difficulties	12 mins.
	40 mins.

Class #30   *The Histories,*
                          by **Herodotus**

Summary/Purpose:

This last class of the year will be an appropriate time to review the kinds of skills you and your students have practiced. The overriding issue has been to develop a sensitivity to the fact that different people view themselves, the world, and others from different points of view. Once one becomes aware that people have different viewpoints, two further skills are necessary. The first is to grasp or understand that point of view and the second is to judge it.

Grasping or understanding a point of view first involves trying to imagine the circumstances that would make it plausible for people to have that viewpoint. Do these people, as individuals or nations, live in such a way that how they behave shows that they have responded sensibly to the circumstances they face? Their behavior or customs may be quite different from ours, but their processes of thinking or reasoning, given their circumstances, might be quite recognizable. This does not imply that their response is proper or correct or justified but only that it is not plainly silly or absurd. To grasp something which initially seems strange to us involves trying to imagine the circumstances that would tempt us to act or think similarly.

The second step in grasping another point of view is to try to think from within that point of view. This can be accomplished by trying to look at ourselves from the point of view of other people. A concrete way to do this is to ask ourselves what actions or opinions of ours would appear strange or peculiar to these people. This enables us to notice aspects of ourselves which perhaps we had never noticed before, generally the ones that are so familiar that we never notice them.

This second step enables us to go on to judge between our viewpoint and theirs. Grasping an alien point of view does not imply approving of it. Understanding why a person has a certain belief is a prerequisite for deciding whether we approve or disapprove, agree or disagree. To accomplish this step we must compare the two perspectives, and this will be practiced in this week's session.

The text by Herodotus describes some of the customs of the ancient Persians. They were different from the customs of Herodotus' own people, the Greeks of the fifth century

B.C., and are quite different from ours. Some of the customs Herodotus describes without any judgment; others, such as the custom that a father does not see his son during the first five years of the child's life, he judges favorably. In considering this text, the students should discuss whether they can supply good reasons for the Persian customs and whether they can approve of the last two.

The handout, which should be done after reading the text, will help the students make their own opinions explicit. It asks them to check the Persian customs which they feel make sense. In addition, it also lists some of our customs and asks for their opinion on how the Persians would react to them. For example, we teach boys and girls in the same way. Do they think the Persians would like what we do? Also we think that children should be raised by both parents from birth. Clearly the Persians would probably not like that.

Since this is the last meeting of the year, it would be useful to encourage the students to reflect on how they have changed as a group throughout the year in this class. This should happen in the last ten minutes of the meeting. Do their present customs, that is, how they act in the Touchstones class, differ from the way they behaved at the start of the year?

The Histories, (Student vol., p. 71)
by Herodotus

The customs of the Persians are very different from ours. The Persians have no pictures of the gods, no special temples or churches, and no altars. They think that those people who do have such things are foolish because the Persians believe God is everywhere. When they wish to pray, they climb to the highest mountain tops. A person who goes to worship God never says a prayer for himself alone. He must also pray for the health and success of the ruler, and then for the good fortune of the whole people in which he himself is included.

They give greatest respect to the country nearest to them. Those who live a little farther away are honored somewhat less. Those who live farthest away are considered worthless. Yet no one uses ideas from other peoples' customs as much as the Persians.

Whenever they hear about something new in another country, they right away do the same themselves.

Next to strength and bravery in battle, the greatest respect is paid to a man because he has fathered many sons. From the ages of five to twenty, a boy is carefully taught only three things: to ride, to shoot an arrow from a bow, and to speak the truth. Until a boy is five, he does not ever see his father. This is so the father will not be sad if the boy dies. To my mind, this is a wise rule and so is the next difference between them and us.

The ruler cannot put anyone to death for only a single fault or crime, no matter what it is. In every such case, the good a person did is compared with the bad. If the bad is greater than the good, then the person is punished. They also hold that it is against the law to talk about anything which it is unlawful to do. The worst thing in the world, they think, is to tell a lie. The second worst is to owe someone money, because a person who owes money must tell lies.

HANDOUT FOR CLASS #30

1. Which of the Persian customs make sense to you?

	makes sense to me	doesn't make sense
a. Persians have no churches.	☐	☐
b. Persians pray on mountain tops.	☐	☐
c. Persians don't respect nations far away from them.	☐	☐
d. Persians most respect a man who has many sons.	☐	☐
e. Persian boys only learn to ride, shoot an arrow, and tell the truth.	☐	☐
f. Persian boys under 5 don't see their father.	☐	☐
g. Persian kings cannot execute anyone for just one crime.	☐	☐

2. Below are some of our nation's customs. Which ones would the Persians like?

	Persians Like	Persians don't like
a. We teach boys and girls the same things.	☐	☐
b. People can pray however they wish.	☐	☐
c. We most respect nations that are free like us.	☐	☐
d. We tend to respect people who help others.	☐	☐
e. We don't mind what people say; what they do matters most.	☐	☐
f. We let people owe money.	☐	☐
g. Children are raised by both parents from birth.	☐	☐

ACTIVITIES FOR CLASS #30

1. Ask the students to sit in a circle. Read the text to them, having them read it silently. Pass out the handout and have them check answers to both questions.

2. Break them into small groups and have them share answers to #1 and #2 and come to a consensus on what customs the Persians would like. They may well disagree over (c), as nothing in the text explicitly says how the Persians feel about freedom.

3. Reconvene in one large circle and have the small groups report on their answers to question #2. Allow for general discussion on these answers. Reserve the last minutes of class time for all to discuss whether the customs or habits they now have in Touchstones discussions are different from how they behaved at the beginning of the year.

(These times are approximate only)

1. Form circle; read text, and answer questions	5 mins.
2. Small-group work	10 mins.
3. Large group: small-group reports, discussion	15 mins
4. Discuss Touchstone customs	<u>10 mins.</u>
	40 mins.